TREASURE
in Jars of Clay

CLAUDIO FREIDZON

TREASURE IN JARS OF CLAY by Claudio Freidzon
Published by Creation House
A part of Strang Communications Company
600 Rinehart Road
Lake Mary, Florida 32746
www.creationhouse.com

Unless otherwise noted, all Scripture quotations are from the Holy
Bible, New International Version. Copyright © 1973, 1978, 1984,
International Bible Society. Used by permission.

Scripture quotations marked KJV are from the
King James Version of the Bible.

Scripture quotations marked NLT are from the Holy Bible, New Living
Translation, copyright © 1996. Used by permission of Tyndale House
Publishers, Inc., Wheaton, IL 60189. All right reserved.

Scripture quotations marked AMP are from the Amplified Bible. Old
Testament copyright © 1965, 1987 by the Zondervan Corporation. The
Amplified New Testament copyright © 1954, 1958, 1987 by the
Lockman Foundation. Used by permission.

Scripture quotations marked NAS are from the New American Standard
Bible. Copyright © 1960, 1962, 1963, 1968, 1971, 1972, 1973, 1975,
1977 by the Lockman Foundation. Used by permission.

Library of Congress Cataloging-in-Publication Data
Freidzon, Claudio.
    [Tesoro en vasos de barro. English]
    Treasure in jars of clay / by Claudio Freidzon.
        p. cm.
    ISBN 0-88419-644-5
    1. Christian life. I. Title.
BV4501.2.F761413 1999
248.4—dc21   99-37519
                                                           CIP

Previously published as *Tesoro en Vasos de Barro*
by Caribe/Betania, a division of Thomas Nelson, Inc.,
copyright © 1999, ISBN 0-88113-411-2.
English translation by Silvia Cudich.
0 1 2 3 4 5 6 7 BBG 9 8 7 6 5 4 3 2
Printed in the United States of America

To . . .

- Betty—for being more than an excellent wife...you are an instrument of God.

- My daughter, Daniela—you are in the flower of your youth, and you are everything I could have ever desired!

- My son Sebastián—strong and courageous. God has prepared great things for you! I have learned to enjoy your fellowship and friendship.

- My son Ezequiel—our youngest. You are the reason for my tenderness and my laughter.

- Every one of the brethren at the King of Kings Church (Iglesia Rey de Reyes)—I could not imagine what my life would be without you. I love you with all my heart, and it is a pleasure and a great honor to be your pastor.

- Every King of Kings Church ministry member—thank you for sharing the battles and victories of God's work with me and for carrying forward the multiplying vision that God has given us for Argentina.

- My Lord, my Potter—I will praise you forever for your faithfulness as you deal with me, a simple jar of clay.

Acknowledgments

- My great friend Carlos Mraida, whose support and strength encouraged me and allowed this book to become a reality.
- Marcelo Doynel, whose tireless help made this new project possible.
- Every King of Kings Church member that participated by writing his or her life testimony and contributed to glorify God in this book.

Introduction

IN THESE LAST years, God, in His infinite grace and mercy, has given me the privilege of serving Him as a preacher, speaking in many important international conferences, and as an evangelist, ministering to thousands of individuals in crusades. Besides ministering in the most important cities in my own country of Argentina, I have been invited to do the same in many countries all over the world—Uruguay, Chile, Ecuador, Brazil, El Salvador, Costa Rica, United States of America, Canada, Spain, Germany, Switzerland, Italy, Hungary, Czechoslovakia, Austria, England, Burkina Faso, Congo, Japan and Australia. This ministry to the nations has a very important place in my service to God, and through it the Lord has allowed me to reach a million and a half people.

Without ceasing to thank God for this privilege, and recognizing the impact this projection has, I want, through this book, to open my heart and share my burden with you. The book that is now in your hands has been written with a pastor's heart. My heart cries when I see so many brothers and sisters in Christ who, in spite of having all they need to live the abundant life, live without that abundance. Believers who have experienced the redeeming work of Christ in their lives, who have received the powerful breath of the Holy Spirit, who have been flooded by the love of our heavenly Father, and yet who go through life without living life to the fullest.

They know the Lord, but their lives need to be restored. At the same time, along with the burden I feel for those who need to experience the restoring work of God, there is great hope and excitement in my heart, knowing that God continues searching for men and women who want to benefit from His grace. In this book you will not only perceive the burden and the strength coming from my pastor's heart, but you will also sense God's heartbeat lovingly saying, "I'm ready to restore you."

What is your image of God? If you had to choose a figure to illustrate God, which one would you choose? Some people see Him as a judge ready to condemn. Others see Him as a policeman ready to suppress. Others imagine Him as a little old man with a long white beard. How do you see Him?

At a very special time in the history of God's people, the Lord decided to stimulate the prophet Jeremiah's imagination so he would conceive God as a potter. If you had to choose an image symbolizing God's actions, you wouldn't probably select that of a potter. However, I'm convinced that this is a time when the church as the believers in Jesus Christ need to recover a vision of God as the Potter. Many believers have opened themselves to the wonderful work of the Holy Spirit and have experienced His transforming anointing. But as time goes by, for different reasons the oil has stopped running, the new wine has turned old, the experience hasn't been renewed and there's a clamor everywhere for restoration.

If this is your situation, the Lord, with His characteristic sweetness and strength, is inviting you today to "Go down to the potter's house" (Jer. 18:1).

This is the word that came to Jeremiah from the LORD: *"Go down to the potter's house, and there I will give you my message." So I went down to the potter's house, and I saw him working at the wheel. But the pot he was shaping from the clay was marred in his hands; so the potter formed it into another pot, shaping it as seemed best to him.*

Then the word of the LORD *came to me: "O house of Israel, can I not do with you as this potter does?" declares the* LORD. *"Like clay in the hand of the potter, so are you in my hand, O house of Israel."*

—JEREMIAH 18:1—6

those circumstances, in that moment, right there in the mud, *God found you and began His work in you.* Blessed be the name of the Lord!

We are as clay, and although many assume we have no value at all, that is not the belief of the Potter. If other people have despised you, be assured that in His hands you will reach your glorious destiny.

I would like to tell you Mario's story. He was a young man who experienced rejection and was abandoned by those whom he loved the most. But one day, out of the mire, the Potter picked him up as a most beautiful treasure.

I was born in Chile, and during my childhood I lived with my father, my mother, my oldest brother Raúl and Luis, the youngest of the family, who had health problems. He was very weak, and my mother had to care for him constantly. My father was an alcoholic and would violently beat us. We were terrified of him. My head and body still show the scars of his beatings. Every night when I heard him coming home, I would experience intense fear and run to hide under the bed.

The situation was more than my mother could endure, so she left, taking little Luis with her. But I stayed behind with my father, who used to vent all his anger and frustration on me. As a five-year-old child, I was powerless, and so I ran "not a people" to become a people.

God has taken you from the clay. Never forget this truth! He grabbed you from the soil, from the place where you had fallen due to your rebelliousness and disobedience, and started to work on you. He didn't refrain from getting His hands into the clay! He didn't look at you expecting to find perfection. He knew He wouldn't find any. He leaned forward, picked you up and put you on the wheel. He is now molding you according to His purposes, forming Jesus in your life and filling you with blessings so that you may go and bless those around you. *But don't ever forget the place from which He took you.*

As the psalmist remembers God's benefits, he says that the Lord redeemed our life "from the pit" (Ps. 103:4). When you were in the pit of depression, He stretched out His arm and rescued you. When love was a word you had to look up in the dictionary because you didn't know its meaning, He came to you and filled you with His unconditional love. When your sins and your guilt wouldn't allow you to lift up your head and have a relationship with Him, He washed you clean and forgave all your sins. When your life had no meaning, He filled your emptiness inside. When peace was just a word and not a reality, God took hold of you and gave rest to your soul. When you were in bondage to that enslaving addiction, wallowing in the mud, He came to you, broke the chains and set you free. There, in the people and with Jeremiah's life as a prophet.

The Lord wants to invite you, through this book, to His workshop. He wants to reveal to you what He wants to do with your life by shaping you according to the specific purposes He has for you. Open your heart and be ready to receive Him!

FROM THE CLAY

In verse 6 of Jeremiah 18, we read, "Like clay in the hand of the potter, so are you in my hand, O house of Israel."

By this illustration God reveals Himself as the potter and declares us to be the clay that He shapes in His hands. Many say, "I will turn to God as soon as I'm OK, whenever I'm ready to come into His presence." But the Word of God says that He called us when we were still far away, lost in our sins. We have to understand this well: It is God who searches for us and chooses us, and He doesn't choose us because we are perfect or good. He doesn't choose you because you are a good father or a good mother or a good neighbor or a good worker. No, He chooses us knowing that we are but clay. The Word says He chose Israel because the people were "not a people." He didn't choose them because of their merits or because of their qualities as a nation. They actually didn't exist as a nation. They were just a group of slaves in Egypt. And yet, God made those that were

Jars of Clay

WHEN A BABY is placed before a mirror, he doesn't recognize himself. He stares and enjoys the image he sees. He smiles at it without knowing that it is his own image. But one day, his expression changes because he starts to recognize his figure and his movements. His face seems to be saying, "That's me." That is what happens to us as we read the story of the potter and the jar. In the beginning we read it as a nice illustration that has nothing to do with us. But as time goes by, the revelation of the Holy Spirit causes our expression to change, and we are forced to say, "That's me; that jar is me."

In His Word God illustrates in a very simple and enlightening way how He deals with us. The image is of the prophet Jeremiah going to the potter's workshop to receive a dramatic teaching from God. There the Lord shows him what He wants to do with bringing the message of forgiveness and salvation to her whole family. All that the devil had tried to destroy forever, the Lord, in His mercy, had restored.

Today, Mario is a joyful and pleasant person. He has a unique sensibility toward the needs of those who, for different reasons, have grown up without the love of others. Because he was rescued, transformed and comforted by God, he can now comfort others.

Mario, along with his wife, shares his testimony in the streets, the hospitals and with marginalized people, whom he wholeheartedly helps. But his number one concern is children. He has a special love for defenseless children since he once was one of them. He visits orphanages periodically to bring the children, in the midst of their misery, all the love and the comfort that God has laid upon his heart.

Praise the Lord! He searched for us in the mire and didn't leave us there. The Scriptures say: "Brothers, think of what you were when you were called. Not many of you were wise by human standards; not many were influential; not many were of noble birth. But God chose the foolish things of the world to shame the wise; God chose the weak things of the world to shame the strong. He chose the lowly things of this world and the despised things—and the things that are not—to nullify the things that are, so that no one may boast before him" (1 Cor. 1:26–29).

become my wife. She could understand me because she also came from a broken home. Her mom had left her, and her grandmother had raised her. She didn't see her mother for years, and so her feelings of abandonment ran deep.

After Clara and I were married, my mother took me to an evangelistic crusade by Pastor Claudio Freidzon in Plaza Noruega. There the Lord healed my spinal problems, which had gotten much worse. I accepted Christ a year later, and a miracle took place. How can I explain it? I felt God's love running through my whole life—past and present. Changes started to occur. A burden was lifted from my shoulders. I was able to forgive my mom with all my heart. I could look into her eyes as if nothing had happened between us. I learned to love her and to understand her. After all, I wasn't the only one who had suffered. It was a real challenge to visit my grandparents and uncles, but after much praying I went to see them. I asked their forgiveness for my resentment, and I offered to forget it all. The impact of the change in me was so great that they surrendered to Jesus and confessed Him as Lord and Savior. During this trip, God gave me another gift. After thirty years, I met my oldest brother Raúl again. It was beautiful to hug him and tell him about God's love. Also, Clara, my wife, had the joy of and I couldn't understand why.

One day as I was walking through a dark alley, I saw a woman walking toward me...It was my mom! I was dirty, my clothes were ragged and I was eight years older than when she left. But she recognized me and took me with her. I went to live with her and with my stepfather and stepsister.

Finally I had a home. But I started having health problems. They were the cruel effects of my terrible childhood, of being cold, hungry, sleepless and beaten. My health was seriously affected, especially my spine. I was all bent and could barely walk. By then, I lived in Argentina, where I had surgery. I spent a year and a half in the Rivadavia Hospital suffering with incredible pain.

Gradually I started to get better and tried to lead a normal life. Just when I finally thought things were getting better, I became terribly depressed. I often thought of killing myself. I actually tried to do it three times.

In those days, my mother and stepfather came to know the Lord, and my mother started to tell me about God's love. Inexplicably, the love I felt for my mom became hatred and resentment. "Don't talk to me about love after abandoning me for so many years," I said.

Around that time I met Clara, who would later

to my grandparents and then to my uncles for help, but they all rejected me. So I decided to run away. For the next four years, the streets became my home. Hungry and cold, eating what I could get, I would sleep on trains or in parks. After a while, tired of living this way, I decided to go back to my father, but it was too late—he had died of cirrhosis. It seemed like too many hardships for a nine-year-old. I decided to see my grandparents and uncles once more, but I was rejected again. They didn't want to take care of me. They convinced me to go to a "good place," where, according to what they said, I would receive an education and help to become a good man. My hopes were raised, not really knowing what awaited me there. When I arrived at that place, I was informed that there were no vacancies left, so they took me to a prison that operated as an orphanage. It was horrible. Violence, torture and screams at night asking for mercy tormented my ears and weighed down my soul. I was so scared I couldn't sleep. I was raped twice. No, definitely this wasn't what they had promised me it would be.

When I turned thirteen, I ran away with three other boys. I walked aimlessly for twenty days. I was totally lost....I was only a boy, but my life wasn't a normal life. My innocence was lost; I had no home; my whole life was painful;

I live a new life. My inner peace is so great that no one will ever be able to take it away from me.

As the Word says, God took us out of the mud and lifted us up to heavenly places. He seated us with Christ so we can live, not wallowing in the mud anymore, but in the fullness of His presence, seated at the right hand of the Father, with all the blessings, all the authority and all the power of Jesus Christ.

The Potter will not be able to do His work in us until we are ready to acknowledge that we are nothing but clay. He can't do anything with those who think they are somebody. The Potter is looking for a piece of soft clay with which to create His masterpiece. People like Mario and Elvira, who have suffered tragedies, are not the only clay. May God allow the rich of this world to realize that they are also clay; the successful, proud and self-righteous to realize that they are clay and their lives are without purpose away from the Potter's hands.

AT THE POTTER'S WHEEL

Salvation—arriving at the Potter's hands—is only the beginning of a great adventure. It is the beginning of a new story.

Jeremiah 18:3 says, "So I went down to the potter's house, and I saw him working at the wheel."

discipleship counselor received me very sweetly. I felt better every day. At home, I would listen to worship music while I cleaned my house, singing and worshiping God. Things didn't look as bad anymore. Soon after, without anyone telling me to, I signed up for a baptism course and got baptized. God was dealing with me.

One Sunday during the main service, the Word of God touched me, and I walked up front in answer to that calling. While the pastor prayed, I felt like I was all alone in the midst of that crowd that was pressing on me from all sides. Just me and God by that altar. Suddenly, during the prayer, I felt lifted up in the air as if hanging from my hands in chains. I heard the pastor's voice saying: "Let go of her, Satan!" I could see my chains breaking. I thought I was in another world, surrounded by a cloud of glory. When I opened my eyes, I was surprised to see so many people around me. God had dealt with me in a very intimate way. I felt restored inside. I was an entirely different person.

Free from hatred and resentment, I started to pray blessings over my mother and my sister. Soon after, I went back to work. My coworkers were surprised to see me, and I would tell them over and over again: "He has told me to come back." When I said "He," meaning the Lord, they thought I meant the company's president.

I had a Christian friend who prayed continually for me. One day, she invited me to an evangelistic meeting led by Pastor Claudio Freidzon in the Sarmiento Park. The first day, I didn't understand what it was all about, but I listened to the Word of God. When Pastor Claudio prayed for me, I was filled with peace, and I was able to sleep that night. On the next Sunday, my friend convinced me to go back. Once again the pastor prayed for me, saying, "Receive what God has for you." I immediately felt a need to leave that auditorium. I suddenly started to cry and cry. I couldn't stop. I didn't even care what others thought of me. I was crying like never before in my life.

A young assistant came and asked me what was going on. "I'm sorry," I said, "I don't know what's going on. I just can't stop crying."

"Don't worry," he said, "you are crying for all those things you were never able to cry for before." I was astounded. How did he know? He continued by saying, "But finally your time has come. The Lord has called you; you have answered; and you will stay forever with Him because He is blessing you." Then he asked to be excused and left. I never saw him again, but his words left a strange peace in my heart. It was as if all the bad things had been erased from my mind and my heart.

I started attending King of Kings Church. A

repair. At that point, I had changed my mind, but I couldn't go back.

When we had almost finished painting the house and were ready to move, the unexpected happened. As we ate dinner one night, my mother and sister told me that they were moving *without me.* They said they had always wanted to live by themselves, and if I had any problems with their decision I could sue them. I couldn't believe my ears. I felt so betrayed. They knew they didn't have enough money to buy the house so they had tricked me into helping them to do it.

I told them, "You have forty-eight hours to leave my house. If I come back and find you here, I swear I will kill you both." The pain I felt was so intense, I couldn't even think. I asked my son to help them move. I came back home as my mother was packing her last things—including some of my clothes. Looking into her eyes, I said, "Look at me. When you die and need me to close your eyes, you will die with your eyes open. You will never hurt me again." Then I turned around and left.

The following months were horrible. I fell into a deep depression. I had spent sixty years trying to get my mother to love me, and I felt defeated. I felt sick just at the thought that they lived two blocks away. Not even the desire for revenge would help my depression.

God places us on the wheel and starts to shape us with His hands according to the design He has in His heart from before the foundation of the world.

The wheel symbolizes the place where God deals with us. The Lord molds us on the wheel. In that sense, the wheel is the school of God—all those circumstances that God allows to take place so that the image of Christ is formed in us.

We often feel that we are just spinning on the wheel, with everything out of control around us. We don't see any progress, and we are discouraged. In our confusion, we look downward, trying to find the one responsible for all that movement, trying to identify who is spinning the wheel. *It must be the devil,* we think, but then we discover something astounding. The Potter's foot is moving the wheel! Everything is under His control!

Today we enjoy the positive influence of technological breakthroughs. Thanks to them, we are able to enjoy a more comfortable life. But when applied to the spiritual realm, technology may lead us to the *instant-everything syndrome,* believing that our spiritual growth will take place in an instant, and that God needs to do everything right away. Somebody called it the *microwave syndrome*—sticking God in a microwave oven, pressing two or three buttons and expecting that our answer will come out automatically. Those who expect God to act like instant coffee take offense at God (or at the church or pastor) when

He holds back His answer or is silent.

It is important for us to realize that God is leaving His mark on us as He shapes us at the wheel. He has to shape clay that may be too dry or resistant or hard. We need His touch. He made us all different because each of us has a specific plan here on earth.

MARRED JARS

As you analyze your life, you may see failure or the broken pieces of that man or woman that God had planned you to be. You know that God has a plan for you from before the foundations of the earth, but as you look at your life today, you feel frustrated as you realize that plan has not become a reality.

What will God do? Will He use another man, another woman to take your place in the kingdom? He could do that, but don't despair. There's still time. The Book of Jeremiah says that the potter, instead of going back to the mire to find some more raw materials, took that same broken piece again. Today, He's taking you back to restore His work. He's willing to start all over again. Unlike people who rejected you at your first mistake without giving you a second chance, and who may still bear grudges against you, the Potter lovingly and patiently tells you, "Let's try again." How wonderful!

It is fundamental to our restoration that we identify where we have failed, the place where we have resisted His will. Let's think about this: Everything went well until the potter reached a point, a crack or an imperfection that prevented him from doing his work. A resistance that didn't give in, causing the vessel to break in his hands.

There are many Christians who have failed. There are many broken jars, jars that can only serve for decoration and many other empty jars. There are jars that instead of being jars of glory are becoming jars of dishonor. The Word says that the Lord in His mercy is willing to put them back on the wheel to make new ones. "But the pot he was shaping from the clay was marred in his hands; so the potter formed it into another pot, shaping it as seemed best to him" (Jer. 18:4). God has started His work in you, and He will bring it to completion.

I want to challenge you in the name of the Lord to be a part of God's moving at this time, a part of the revival that He will bring to Argentina and to other parts of the world. Stop being a broken jar. Stop being a jar just sitting on a shelf for decoration, a Christian stuck in a temple. Let God change you into a jar of mercy that can be taken to those in need to spread God's love among them. Be a jar that expresses God's glory here on earth!

RETURN TO THE POTTER'S HANDS

God concludes by saying, "O house of Israel, can I

not do with you as this potter does?...Like clay in the hand of the potter, so are you in my hand, O house of Israel" (Jer. 18:6). Let the Holy Spirit grab your imagination. Take Jeremiah's hand, and go into the Potter's house. You can watch Him working at the wheel. He is working on a jar of clay; that jar is your life. But you can see that jar is marred in His hands. You can probably explain why God's purposes are not being fulfilled in your life. You could spend the rest of your life making excuses and blaming others or the circumstances. But the truth is that the jar is marred, and God's work is not fulfilled yet.

Now, look at that jar, your own life, broken, fragmented, marred, half-finished, in the Potter's hands, and listen to Him saying, "I will make a better jar according to My will. I want to do it." Can you trust in His love? Can you trust in His power?

No matter how far you are from His will, return to the Potter's hands!

So the potter formed it into another pot, shaping it as seemed best to him.

—JEREMIAH 18:4

2

Hopeless Jars

THE FIRST STEP to allowing the Potter to work in our lives is to recognize our need of restoration. When a work of art cracks or peels, it is sent to an expert who will repair it and restore it to its original state. As we have seen, our sin resists the Potter's work and prevents us from becoming that unique piece that God intends us to be. Our faults scrape, peel, crack and even break the vessel, which is our life. But our Potter and Creator is an expert Restorer. He is always ready to lay His hands on us to restore us to our original purpose.

But we have to acknowledge our need first. We have to cry out to God and ask to be restored. This is not the cry of pharisaic Christians who think they don't need restoration, pretending they are perfect. This is the cry of those who don't hide behind a mask.

In Psalm 80, Asaph, the worship leader of God's

people, prayed for himself and his people, asking for their restoration. The same Holy Spirit that inspired Asaph to pray these words will enlighten and lead you to pray for the restoration of your life.

THE CRY OF THE AFFLICTED

Psalm 80 contains a deep cry. It isn't just a nice song—it is a testimony, a cry. It is a collective groan, but also an individual one. It is the cry of Asaph, a man who suffers affliction. He recognizes his sin, his situation, and desperately asks, cries and groans. He even repeats his request, his cry and his groan, begging for the restoration of his life.

This is the same cry of the church and of many believers today. It may be your cry as you read this book. It is the prayer of the Christian who feels that his Christian life has fallen apart, his relationship with God has grown cold and powerless, sin has settled in and communion with God is just not the same anymore. God seems far away, removed from his life.

The cry of Asaph is the cry of one who feels that in having strayed away from God, he has lost God's protection. "Why have you broken down its walls so that all who pass by pick its grapes?" (v. 12). The walls that protected his life have broken down; the protective fences are broken. It began with a cooling off, followed by sin. Now, with the walls broken down, he is exposed to Satan's attacks.

This is the cry of one who feels that his grapes are being plucked, that the fruit of the vine in his Christian life are being picked. All he has left are the memories of personal experiences with the Lord, of beautiful moments together, of spiritual growth and an awareness of the great love God has for him.

I have encountered brothers in the faith who have told me, "Pastor Claudio, in 1992 I went to your church, and you prayed for me, and my life was radically changed. But then, as time went by, I drifted; I didn't renew the work of the Spirit in my life. Today I need a new touch of God to restore me."

Asaph's cry was dramatic: "Boars from the forest ravage it and the creatures of the field feed on it" (v. 13). It is the cry of one who feels that the beasts of the field have come in to destroy the vine. He knows that the dirty and unclean are destroying his life. He senses that the devil is like a roaring lion seeking to destroy him. But since the walls are down and the fences have been broken, he doesn't know what to do. He sees God as far away, angry and unwilling to listen.

In frustration, he prays: "Return to us, O God Almighty! Look down from heaven and see!" (v. 14). If God doesn't listen, life is nothing but tears: "You have fed them with the bread of tears; you have made them drink tears by the bowlful" (v. 5).

It is the cry of one who feels that his enemy mocks him and ridicules him because of his situation: "And our enemies mock us" (v. 6). It is the groan of one who feels that his life is like a ravaged, burned and cut-down vine. So today with Asaph we lift our cry, our clamor, our groan, our request, our prayer: "Restore us, O God; make your face shine upon us, that we may be saved" (v. 3; cf: 7, 19). O God, restore us!

THE CRY OF ONE WHO REMEMBERS
HOW IT USED TO BE

Psalm 80 is not the request of an unbeliever. It is the expression of a person who remembers so perfectly how different his life used to be. The psalmist remembers how God rescued him and drove the enemy out of his life: "You brought a vine out of Egypt; you drove out the nations and planted it" (v. 8). It is the desperate cry of one who has known God's love, freedom and salvation.

It is not a request made by an immature and unstable Christian. It is the prayer of a Christian who has been planted by God and has roots. It is not a passive Christian's plea. It is the cry of a son of God who remembers that his life used to bear fruit, that his work for the Lord was blessed: "The mountains were covered with its shade, the mighty cedars with its branches. It sent out its boughs to the Sea, its shoots as far as the River" (vv. 10–11). It is not the request of a self-centered Christian. It is the cry of one whose life gave care and protection to the weak and needy in its shade, and whose words brought hope to those in despair.

Please! Don't think that Psalm 80 is just a request—it is the cry and groan of one who has experienced God and tasted His love and been saved and delivered by Him. It talks to us about a person who has set down roots and grown spiritually, bearing fruit and being a blessing to others. It is precisely because he knows what God has done in his life, because he remembers his relationship with Him and its outcome, that he raises this prayer: "O God, restore us! Make Your face shine upon us and we will be saved. Help us to be what we used to be. Look with favor on us, and we will be safe. O God, restore us!"

THE CRY OF ONE WHO KNOWS GOD

Psalm 80 is not the petition of a person who doesn't know God. On the contrary, it is the clamor of the one who knows Him very well. It is the cry of the Christian who, precisely because he knows who God is, is aware of the resources that are available to him. We will not find as many names and attributes of God in other Bible passages as in this one. For example, in verses 4 and 19, three names are mentioned, one next to the other, emphasizing who God is: "LORD God Almighty" incorporates the three Hebrew names of God—*Yahweh, Elohim, Sebaot.*

It is, therefore, the cry of the one who knows that God is *Yahweh,* of him who understands the expression: "I AM WHO I AM." It is the clamor of the one who knows that God is the Being, the very existence, the only one who can give us life. That is why in verse 18 we read: "Revive us."

It is also the cry of the one who knows that God is *Elohim.* This name speaks of His power, excellence and majesty. It is the clamor of the one who knows that God is King and Lord. He prays because he knows that He is sovereign, holding all authority, ruler of everything.

And it is also the cry of the one who knows that God is *Sebaot,* God of hosts, captain of the heavenly hosts, of angels and of His church.

This psalm is also the prayer of the one who knows that the Lord is *Israel's Shepherd.* The psalmist asks to be shepherded, led and heard by Him since he knows that the Lord is a God who is close to us (v. 1).

It is the cry of one who knows that God is holy. That is why he asks God to shine forth (v. 1). It is the groan of one who knows that God saves us and doesn't condemn us. That is why in verse 2 it says: "Awaken your might; come and save us."

It is the groan of one who knows that God is a merciful God. That is why he asks Him to set aside His anger (v. 4) and to look at him with favor, smiling, with a shining face (v. 3).

Don't make mistakes. It isn't the plea of one who approaches God without knowing Him. It is the cry of the one who knows Him perfectly. The only reason he

cries out to Him in desperation is because he knows that He is the only one who can renew him and give him life. He knows that He is the Lord and King of the universe; He has power and majesty; He is the only Shepherd able to lead him back to his path. He is the only three-times Holy One, whose light illuminates his life. He knows that He is the only Savior, full of love and mercy, able to rescue him and ready to give him a second chance, the one who is close and listening. "O God, restore us! Make Your face shine upon us and we will be saved. Help us to be what we used to be. Look with favor on us and we will be safe. O God, restore us!"

THE CRY FOR RESTORATION

Asaph, Israel's worship leader, lifted this prayer up to the Lord, telling Him what you need to tell Him today. He asks God to return to him, to come back (v. 14); not because God had left him—rather because he moved away from God. Now he needs God to be back in his life.

He tells God to look with favor upon him, to make His face shine upon him, to smile (v. 3). He asks Him not to look at the sin and to measure him with love, not with justice. His prayer is that God may watch over the vine that His hand has planted (v. 14).

Asaph reminds God that Israel, as His people, and he as an individual, are the root He has planted, the

branch He has raised up for Himself, to have intimacy with Him (v. 15). He prays that His hand will rest on him (v. 17). Finally, full of hope, he declares that God will revive him (v. 18).

Asaph told God exactly what we have to tell Him today: "Lord, return now, come back, look with favor on us. Have mercy and visit me again. I am the plant that You planted so lovingly. I am the branch that You raised up for Yourself. Don't forget about me; may Your hand be upon me and give me life."

God is giving you this psalm today. It is for you who have already experienced God's salvation, love and power. He had anointed you in the past; you bore fruit, and your work in His name had spread. And yet you are not living that abundance today. You need to renew your communion with Him. You need His anointing to be fresh and powerful in you again.

God gave me this psalm for you today. I want to support you spiritually. I want both of us to cry to the Lord, saying: "O God, restore us! Make Your face shine upon us, and we will be saved. Help us to be what we used to be. Look with favor on us, and we will be safe. O God, restore us! O God, restore us! O God, restore us!"

The psalmist ends with a promise in verse 18: "Then we will not turn away from you." This is the promise you must make today: "Lord, restore me so that I will not turn away from You. But first, Lord, restore me, and help me to be the same as I used to

be. Restore me, Lord; anoint me once again."

Maybe it was just a scratch or a crack that happened to your jar. Maybe the damage seems big and beyond repair. It may seem unusable. But the distance between your situation and the Restorer is just a prayer. If He sees that your honest intentions are never to turn away from Him again, He will take you in His hands once more and make you into a new jar, shaping you as seems best to Him.

Take a step to overcome the distance by saying this prayer with me:

> *Lord, You are my Potter. I come to You to be restored. I trust in Your unlimited power and Your infinite love for me. That is why I ask You to restore me.*
>
> *Make me the one I once used to be. Look with favor on me, and I will be the same again. Cleanse me with the blood of Christ, and anoint me with the power of the Holy Spirit. Restore my ministry so that I may bear fruit.*
>
> *I pray that through me Your kingdom may reach the ends of the earth. O Lord, restore me, and I will never turn away from You. In the name of Jesus. Amen.*

Though ye have lien among the pots, yet shall ye be as the wings of a dove covered with silver, and her feathers with yellow gold.

—PSALM 68:13, KJV

3

Fragmented Jars

WE ARE ENTERING into the great harvest time—the harvest of lives rescued for Christ. Our challenge, our vision, is to see our city changed and our country transformed. God wants to use your life and your church for that incredible harvest, for that special outpouring of the Holy Spirit. He wants to use you and your congregation as vehicles for the transformation of your city and of your nation.

When you hear or read about the revival that is sweeping over entire nations, when you receive the prophetic word that the time of the outpouring of the Holy Spirit has come, you may say, "I would like to be part of the move of the Spirit and bring thousands of people to the feet of Christ." Perhaps, along with this desire, you immediately think of all your inadequacies that could prevent revival from happening. You may possibly find

some obstacles in your life that would stop you from feeling a part of this revival or from being part of the great harvest.

TWO OBSTACLES IN YOUR LIFE

There are at least two major obstacles that can prevent revival from happening. Most believers have one of these obstacles. It prevents them from freely serving the Lord and from being a part of the move of the Spirit today.

The first obstacle is to feel defeated. Feelings of inadequacy, of incompetence and of unworthiness are the first things that hold us back. Many people feel that they don't have the courage or the necessary conditions to meet the challenge of revival.

The second obstacle is unresolved suffering—the inability to find an explanation for our past and present suffering. Most people have suffered a lot in the past or are going through trials and difficulties in the present. Because of past or present pain, they are focused on their problems, and they can't see beyond their own difficulties. It is impossible for them to see other people's needs or the needs of their city or country. Their spiritual eyes need to be opened. The scales need to fall from their eyes, and the veil needs to be removed so that they can see God's plan—not just for their own lives, but for the rest of the people.

The passage at the beginning of this chapter says: "Though ye have lien among the pots, yet shall ye be as the wings of a dove covered with silver, and her feathers with yellow gold." The verbs used in this text speak of two different tenses. There is something that has already taken place in the past—"ye have lien among the pots"—and something that will take place in the future—"ye shall be as the wings of a dove covered with silver, and her feathers with yellow gold."

It is important to consider both facts: what has already occurred and what God wants to do in your life.

YOUR LIFE IS LIKE A JAR OF CLAY

Jars of clay—the pots, vessels and jars that were made out of clay—were shaped for different purposes. Such jars of clay, precisely because of the material from which they were made, often had very little monetary value. Through this figure the psalmist refers to the experience of many people who were considered as valueless and worthless as jars of clay, thrown there among the broken pots.

As a pastor I have frequently helped people who have felt this way as a result of their experiences of rejection and abandonment. I would like to tell you some of their stories:

No father's love

I was born into a Christian home, but unfortunately my parents separated when I was only four months old. I grew up without my father's love. My mother raised me, and being a single mom, she made many mistakes. I suffered much. She didn't mean to mistreat me, but she did, and I harbored all those things in my heart. I grew up without a hug, without a kiss, without telling my mother I loved her, and as a result, I felt really bad inside. The Lord started to deal with that part of me. I was like a broken vessel, not able to hold anything inside. I would pray, "Lord, use me," but I didn't believe He could.

When I was a little girl, even though I couldn't see Him, He was always there, protecting and preserving me for Himself.

While we prayed at church one night, I felt that Jesus was holding my hands and saying, "In spite of your bad times, I've always been with you."

I told the Lord, "Heal me; I want to serve You, but I don't know how to do it. I get up but I fall down again. I feel useless." At that very moment, I felt the Lord's embrace, and I was able to forgive my father and mother with all my heart. I am a different person now.

Rejection

Some people experience rejection from the very beginning of their lives. Eventually, they believe that they are worthless. If their parents can't love them, how could others? A lady shared this with us:

> I come from a broken home. My parents threw me out of the house when I was only ten years old. My mother was an alcoholic, and my father led a double life, having another wife and children. Even though I hated and cursed my mother, the Lord helped me to love her. I resented being her daughter and belonging to such an evil family with such unloving parents. They never hugged me or kissed me. I never heard the words "I love you" coming from their lips.
>
> The Lord dealt with me, and I was able to forgive my mother who had rejected me. I feel as though I can love her now. I can come to her and give her a kiss without any feelings of rejection inside of me.

We all need our parents to love us, praise us and encourage us in positive ways. We need their protection and even their forgiveness. We need to know that they love us just as we are and that they will always give us a second chance. These are basic needs, and we can never get enough of them.

When we come into the world as vulnerable babies, we are like empty vessels in need of being filled with love and tender care. In this sense, our parents and families have a unique responsibility. Unfortunately, in many cases our jars have not been filled sufficiently, leaving us hurting and incapable of giving to others what we ourselves haven't received.

Resentment

This same truth helps us to understand and forgive our parents. They cannot give us what they themselves have not received. Do you know the backgrounds of your parents' families, their stories?

The Lord dealt with a young man's heart that was full of resentment toward his parents. "They never loved me. They were harsh and distant," he remembered painfully. But during a time of prayer the Lord changed his perspective. God showed him his parents' childhood. He saw them as they arrived in Argentina, running away from the war in Europe. He was reminded of his father's selling newspapers on the streets to help out his family, even though he was only a child. He saw him standing on the street on cold winter mornings, very shabbily dressed, offering newspapers for sale. He also remembered his mother's tough childhood, full of hardship and pain.

He not only forgave them, but he also asked the Lord to forgive him for having resented them. In a

moving, public church meeting, he asked his parents to forgive him and told them how much he loved them.

Forgiveness is not a matter of denying the fact that we have been hurt. When we understand that our parents didn't give us what they themselves didn't receive, we are able to forgive. God provides us with the opportunity to break the generational chains. He wants to fill us to overflowing with His perfect love, so that we may also love others in need.

Repetitive cycles

A lady in our church recognized that she was projecting her own family's history, which was full of deprivation, to her own children. She told us:

The day I understood what the Bible means by forgiveness, my eyes were opened to a different reality. I used to say, "Lord, in spite of his leaving me and his indifference, I've already forgiven my girls' father." But as I prayed, the Holy Spirit reminded me that I hadn't hugged or kissed my daughters in nine years. I remembered how sad I felt when someone called me a "single mom." As a single at church I would see the couples there and ask, "Why not me?" I had a father who didn't love me, and now I had no husband. Why did I always have to be alone?

Whenever rejection was mentioned, I would

pray, "Lord, I'm at home; I work; I take care of my daughters; I'm mother and father to them—why don't I have a husband at my side?" So God started to deal with me. He filled me with His love and freed me from all dependence on men. He is my Beloved, my all!

At the same time, my eyes were opened to the reality facing my daughters. I had to admit painfully that I had burdened them with part of my pain and frustration. When the oldest was born, it took me two days to hold her; I rejected her because I wanted a boy. I thought my youngest was so ugly that I had to hide her away. After this time I've had with God, all I want to do now is to go home and ask their forgiveness. I want to hug them and love them.

Inferiority

We need other people's love so much, and yet so often we don't get it. We feel worthless, thrown among the pots. Another lady told us the following story:

The Lord brought something to light that had been hidden away since I was a child. When others said, "We are special and unique and unique in God's eyes," I would say *amen,* but I never really believed it. I have been a Christian for three and a half years, and God has now helped me to understand where my inferiority is coming from. My sisters were very controlling. They used to be in charge of everything, and that made me feel alienated and insecure. The Lord has shown me that I'm special to Him, that He loves me and that I am the apple of His eye. The heavy chains have broken, and I have a new heart.

At times, even the minor details of everyday life have hurt many. I remember one elderly lady, with tears in her eyes, telling us this:

Because I never knew my mother's love, this ministry time has meant a lot to me. She never combed my hair; I never wanted to sit at the table, and she had to force me to eat my breakfast. She was harsh, distant, cold. The Lord told me, "If I have forgiven her, why can't you?" I have been set free from that pain.

You may be feeling like that. You may have been overlooked in the early years of your life. Possibly you didn't receive the recognition you needed, and therefore you developed an insecure and unstable personality structure, with strong feelings of inferiority. You look at yourself in the mirror and think, *I don't have much value, much significance. I'm simple and ordinary, just one more in the*

41

crowd. I don't stand out or excel. I'm just a pot. Then you lift up your eyes to the heavens and tell the Lord, "If You want to do something valuable in this city or in this nation, You'd better look for somebody else, because I'm no good." You weren't valued enough; you were thrown among the broken pots, and now you feel unworthy, good for nothing. You don't think God could use you for something as big and significant as a revival in your town or in your country.

You may feel frustrated because the circumstances of your life were not positive ones.

I remember clearly the hard years of brokenness in my life. My ministry wasn't getting anywhere. I had come out of seminary full of energy, but the reality of my own limitations became more evident every day. I felt frustrated. I was a shepherd without sheep. For seven long years, my whole congregation consisted of just four sweet old ladies and my family. When it was cold, only my wife, Betty, would come to hear me preach. There were times when my friends, pastors or missionaries would suddenly drop in on the service and find me there all by myself. I would feel like dying. The devil had a weapon. He would whisper in my ears, "You were wrong. You're no good at this; you will never prosper." At times I thought about quitting. I was angry, feeling like a victim and thinking that nobody cared for me. On top of this, our financial situation was terrible. I could hardly feed our family. We lived in an old, broken-down house with no hot water. Our meetings took place right there, in a little room prepared every evening for it. God dealt with me throughout those years and taught me to depend on Him alone.

The Potter wants to restore your life!

A Broken Jar

There is a second obstacle to consider. The word *potsherd* means a pottery fragment. When a jar breaks, each piece is a potsherd. Job 2:8 says that Job took a piece of broken pottery and scraped himself with it as he sat among the ashes. He didn't use a jar to scratch himself; he used a piece of broken pottery. That sharp fragment was useful for getting rid of the itching. Isaiah 30:14 says: "It will break in pieces like pottery, shattered so mercilessly that among its pieces not a fragment will be found for taking coals from the hearth or scooping water out of a cistern." The jar had been so heavily broken that there wasn't a large enough piece to contain a little water from the well or for taking coals from the hearth.

The potsherd is something that has been broken— a cracked jar, a broken vessel—a broken and dry piece of clay. David said, "My strength is dried up like a potsherd, and my tongue sticks to the roof of my mouth; you lay me in the dust of death" (Ps. 22:15).

You may feel like David. You may be convinced that God can't use you. "I'm nothing more than a jar of clay," you say. You believe that God could only glorify Himself through someone more outstanding and valuable. You insist to God, "My life is in pieces. I was thrown among the potsherds. I'm only a fragment of something that broke, of something that never was, of something that was destroyed. I feel like the psalmist—dry. I'm like a dry potsherd. My tongue is stuck to the roof of my mouth, and You have laid me in the midst of ashes. I'm broken. I've been mercilessly destroyed."

Things that take place in a short moment can leave us scarred for the rest of our lives! It is like a ton of bricks suddenly falling on a jar of clay, breaking it into pieces.

Sexual abuse during childhood can scar a person. If it is a woman, she may never be able to trust men again. Or she may reject her husband or even herself. I remember an older lady who was confessing, for the very first time, the sexual abuse she had suffered. The images and sensations were stuck in her mind forever. She rejected her body and couldn't have a normal married life. The abuse itself had lasted only a few seconds, but it had left her confused, angry and humiliated, and its effects lasted forever. Thank God that Jesus Christ, our Healer, came to her and delivered her from the pain.

Adultery—feeling unjustly betrayed by someone

we trusted—breaks the vessel. We need the Master to restore us.

Fraud or financial crisis can leave a family in poverty, producing an inner brokenness, which is very difficult to overcome.

Disappointment, betrayal and negative circumstances have destroyed the jar you used to be, that wonderful vessel, and now it's just potsherds, good only to scratch itching skin. And so you think, *Lord, what revival are You talking about? What blessing for others when I can barely deal with my own life? How are You going to use me for changing a city when I can't solve my own frustration, my own pain?*

Do you feel like that? If so, I want to tell you with the authority the Lord has given to me, that what you are saying has been true, but just until today. That is only part of the story, the story of what happened until today. But there is a second part, which is what God wants to do from this point on in your life.

A DOVE WITH GOLDEN FEATHERS AND SILVER WINGS

What will God do in the future? Read carefully what Psalm 68:13 says: "Ye shall be as the wings of a dove covered with silver, and her feathers with yellow gold" (KJV). The Lord says that He will make you like the wings of a dove covered with silver. In the Bible, silver is a symbol of purification: "Like silver refined in a furnace of clay, purified seven times" (Ps. 12:6). Silver is exposed to intense heat and refined, purified seven times. "For you, O God, tested us; you refined us like silver" (Ps. 66:10).

The psalmist says that the feathers of the dove are covered with gold. Gold symbolizes the costliest metal. For example, the prophet Isaiah says, "I will make man scarcer than pure gold, more rare than the gold of Ophir" (Isa. 13:12). To God, we are the most precious things there are.

In 1 Peter 1:7 we read, "These [trials] have come so that your faith—of greater worth than gold, which perishes even though refined by fire—may be proved genuine and may result in praise, glory and honor when Jesus Christ is revealed." The Lord is saying this: "You have suffered neglect, hardships, trials and pain. I will take hold of all that and will change you into something different. I am going to transform you. You will be like the wings of a dove. Those wings are covered with purified silver and with feathers covered with gold, the most precious metal."

God is showing you the reason why you had to suffer. The Lord shows you the purpose of it all. Your life, like silver, had to be tried by fire. You may be saying, "Pastor Claudio, I've not only been through the fire once, but seven times through. I was tried seven times. Just when I thought I was coming out of a trial, I would enter another. And I'm still in the fire; I'm still in the furnace."

God explains that just as fire refines silver, so our lives are refined by trials. God has a purpose: He wants to make something out of your life. He promises to change you. He will change your feelings of unworthiness and cover you with gold, with the most precious metal there is. That is to say that your life is covered with all the worth God wants to give to it; it is covered with the precious things God has for you.

The change between what we used to be and what God wants us to be now is His sovereign work. It doesn't happen suddenly or by coincidence or because of our destiny. We have to allow God to transform us from potsherds into doves with silver wings, covered with gold. Our almighty God wants you to stop being a piece of pottery lying in a corner. He wants you to start being a dove with silver wings and with feathers covered with gold.

In the Bible the dove symbolizes two things. The dove is a sign of the firstfruits of God's new creation—the symbol of re-creation. The Book of Genesis says that after the flood, when the dove returned to Noah in the evening, there in its beak was a freshly plucked olive leaf! Then Noah knew that the water had receded from the earth. (See Genesis 8:11.) But the dove is also the symbol of the Holy Spirit's actions, of His presence. "As soon as Jesus was baptized, he went up out of the water. At that moment heaven was opened, and he saw the Spirit of God descending like a dove and lighting on him" (Matt. 3:16).

God takes hold of your life and transforms you into the firstfruit of His new creation. The *firstfruit* means the first, His new creation's first work. God first makes you anew. Like the potter, He lays His hands on you and starts to shape you again. He tells you that not everything is lost. Even though you've been discarded among the pots, He picks you up and will shape you into a work of art. It won't be just any jar; He will make a silver dove whose feathers are gold. And He will also do a wonderful work of restoration in your life so that you may become firstfruits of the new creation, of the renewal, the restoration that He will, through the Holy Spirit, bring upon the whole world.

YOUR ROLE IN THE WORK OF GOD

I'm sure that your question right now must be: "What is my role in all this? What do I need to do?" The first thing is to have an attitude of simplicity. Jesus said that we had to be gentle as doves. God wants to change us into doves—simple as doves. We need to have a simple, single-minded and honest attitude before God. With all sincerity, tell the Lord: "Here is my life. I feel like a broken jar, cast out among pieces of clay, among ordinary things, broken, fragmented, crushed. I'm only useful for scratching a miserable itch like Job." Tell him about your brokenness. God first needs your honest heart to bring about a change.

There is a second thing God requires. The dove was the Israelites' simplest offering to God. It was the sacrifice offered by the poor. Those who couldn't offer a lamb or a deer would bring a dove. And so, even though you feel your life isn't worth much and that you're not a lamb or a deer, God wants you to offer Him everything you are as a sacrifice. He wants you to offer yourself like a dove—a white, pure, clean sacrifice, entirely consecrated to Him. Then God will take your life and will transform you into the firstfruits of His new creation, of the harvest He desires to give us, of the revival He wants to breathe over your city. He wants you to carry the presence of the holy Dove, the Holy Spirit, for the blessing of many.

What will you do with your life? Will you be a broken piece of pottery or a dove? I pray that the Lord may transform you into a "dove covered with silver, and her feathers with yellow gold."

Judah mourns, her cities languish; they wail for the land, and a cry goes up from Jerusalem. The nobles send their servants for water; they go to the cisterns but find no water. They return with their jars unfilled; dismayed and despairing, they cover their heads.

—JEREMIAH 14:2–3

4

Empty Jars

THE TEXT IN Jeremiah 14:2–3 clearly describes something that often happens to us. We foresee our objectives and believe that we will achieve that for which we are looking. But as we launch towards the fulfillment of our dreams, we don't find the water that we so much desired. So, we return with empty vessels in our hands. Disillusionment hits, and we are left in a state of shame and confusion. We start to think about what others may say when they see our failure, and so we feel foolish and deeply frustrated. We also experience confusion because we don't understand why we failed, why we were unable to realize our dreams.

We ask God why He allowed us to get into such a mess. We feel terribly depressed. A deep sense of discouragement controls us, and we don't feel like starting all over again or moving on with life. We realize the truth of Proverbs 18:14, which says, "A man's spirit sustains him in sickness, but a crushed spirit who can bear?"

Disillusionment is a truly powerful weapon in Satan's hands. It leads us into depression. It is a universal frustration that we all must face and resolve so that we may have hope in our lives.

LET US CONSIDER DISILLUSIONMENT

To be disappointed is to be unhappy because our hope-filled dreams have failed to materialize. Disillusionment is that despondency we feel when all our plans, dreams and convictions crash before our eyes.

Even though the devil uses the pain of disillusionment to defeat us, I believe that it is a positive thing in our lives. The dictionary defines *disillusionment* as "the loss of dreams, as being disillusioned." If disillusionment helps us to stop living lies or living in a dream world, then it is to be welcomed.

Many people live in a dream world. The word *illusion* comes from a Latin word that means "to deceive." Illusion is an error of the mind or the senses. We perceive appearances as if they were real. The naïve person or the dreamer is a victim of deceit. It is good to feel the pain of disillusionment when you have been the victim of someone's deceit.

Disillusionment is only good if we are able to

understand what our illusion was, if we can understand what kind of deceit we were under. There are six illusions that can deeply hurt believers. Although disillusionment hurts, the real problem lies in the deceit that led you to believe in that dream in the first place. That's why it is important to pay attention to these very common illusions.

Disillusioned with your dreams

The first illusion is to live projected into the future instead of living in the present. There are people who are constantly thinking about tomorrow, making plans, trying to discern God's will for the future, praying only for what is to come. And while they live focused on the future, they mortgage their present. It is good to anticipate things, but if that prevents us from living fully in the present, we are falling into an illusory escape. Instead of facing today's reality, we run away by looking ahead. As a Russian proverb says, "You can't warm a house with the promised firewood."

The anxiety caused by this futuristic attitude fills us with anguish. The Word encourages us to cast all our anxieties on the Lord for He cares for us (1 Pet. 5:7). As a French philosopher once said, "The only thing we can be sure of about tomorrow is that God will rise before the sun."

It is good to plan and organize our life. But if all we do is plan, we will never accomplish anything. It is important to make a plan in order to raise a building. But if all I do is make plans and never start to build, no matter how good my blueprints might be, I will never have a building. There are many believers who only make plans. Every time one talks to them they seem to be working on a new project, but it never comes to pass.

Believers need to know God's will, but many Christians spend their lives wondering, and even asking others, about God's will for the future. And sad to say, while they wonder about the future, they neglect God's will for the present.

Prayer is a wonderful resource. How exciting it is to be able to pray for things in the future. When we pray for what is to come, we get rid of all our worries. But it is sad when the present circumstances remain the same. While we pray for plans and future things, we miss out on the present. Someone once said that life is something that takes place while we are busy planning for the future.

Jesus challenged us to live one day at a time. The only day He gave us to manage and to do His will is *today*. He exhorts us strongly when He says, "Therefore do not worry about tomorrow, for tomorrow will worry about itself. Each day has enough trouble of its own" (Matt. 6:34). Therefore, if you are hurting because your plans didn't come through, welcome the disillusionment. I'm glad you're not deceived anymore. Your projects may be destroyed, but God puts bricks into your hands so that you can start building today.

Disillusioned with your plans

A second illusion is to believe that we can plan our lives by ourselves, without God's intervention. When we become disillusioned, God causes us to question whose plans we were really pursuing—our plans or His?

The pain caused by disappointment is the result of our own illusions and deceits, of building our lives using *our plans* rather than *God's* as the foundation. When we firmly believe and understand this concept, our next step will be to tell the Lord that we don't want to start making our own plans again, that we want to abide by His designs. I will no longer do my will, but God's.

Be aware from now on that what you need most is the fulfillment of God's plan in your life. Are you disillusioned? Have you lost all hope? Don't be afraid. There is something positive in all of this. God is calling you. The failure of your plans is under God's control, and He uses those difficulties to help you understand that you need His plans.

Disillusioned with your idea of happiness

The illusion of believing that our happiness depends upon our dreams becoming a reality is another source of deceit that brings suffering. A letter that I received reflects it very well:

> In the winter of 1991, before carrying out my decision to take my own life and my daughter's, I cried out to God while I was lying on my bed, "God, why did You bring me into this world?" I remember suffering a deep depression caused by disappointments and hopelessness. I felt empty and couldn't see beyond my worries and isolation. I couldn't go on. A dark hand of violence and destruction had shattered all my aspirations about family, marriage, profession and motherhood. That same hand was full of materialism, selfishness, failures and frustrations. I hated my life and believed that the only way out was death.

This is an example of millions of people who look for happiness in good things, relying on their achievements rather than on God's love.

Happiness is much more than the emotion we feel deep in our hearts when our dreams come true. Psychologists explain that desires produce anxiety, and that even when they are fulfilled, sooner or later that anxiety we feel will produce negative results. Life is much more than the emotion we experience when we accomplish something. We can't feed on these emotions. It would be like expecting a child to grow up healthy and strong by eating sweets and candy.

It is a costly mistake to think this way. When success is not achieved, when dreams don't come true, when wishes are not fulfilled, the pain we experience is as strong as the emotions we felt before. We feel unhappy and sad, and nothing in the past is able to compensate for the way we feel now.

A great thinker once said, "He who expects to be happy in the way he imagined it would be, in a certain place with a certain person, ends up in unhappiness. Happiness goes beyond us; it can't be part of our plans. Our plans need to be adapted to God's eternal plan because our happiness comes from Him alone."

Communion with God is our true source of happiness. The psalmist, after much suffering, understood this truth and was able to say:

> Apart from you I have no good thing...I have set the LORD always before me. Because he is at my right hand, I will not be shaken. Therefore my heart is glad and my tongue rejoices; my body also will rest secure...You have made known to me the path of life; you will fill me with joy in your presence, with eternal pleasures at your right hand."
> —PSALM 16:2, 8–9, 11

David declares that he will not be shaken. Nothing will disappoint him because the source of his joy and happiness, his abundant life, is not his dreams, but rather being in the very presence of God. The

Potter has created us to be in His hands. One of the fathers of the church said, "Lord, we have been created for You, and our soul is restless until it rests in You." It is in Him and Him alone where we find real fulfillment and everlasting happiness.

Disillusioned with your need for recognition

A fourth deceptive illusion is to believe that we have to make a name for ourselves, looking everywhere for recognition and approval from others. This attitude is a true source of disillusionment. Many believers lack an abundant life because they are enslaved to other people's opinions. A need for recognition and approval can cause a person to become dependent, able to respond only to other people's expectations and maintain their approval. Tragedy hits when the praise doesn't come, or worse yet, when instead of praise there is criticism. Then disappointment causes reality to hit. But if we look for God's acceptance and unconditional love, and accept others and ourselves as God accepts us, we will never suffer from this illusion again. God's love is an infinite source of acceptance, care and appreciation. We will never be enslaved to others and their opinions anymore.

Disillusioned with the expectation of external changes

Another illusion that will eventually lead to suffering

is to believe falsely that if our circumstances change, then we'll be happy. To believe that my happiness depends on circumstances around me is total foolishness. As if we believed that by using a new racquet, we will become great tennis players. Most Christians spend their prayer time asking God to change their circumstances. Only very few will say, "Lord, change *me*." So they live on standby. They live their lives as if they were on some kind of waiting list. They wait for their boss to change, for their spouse to change, for their mother-in-law to move out of the house, for the government to implement a new health plan—from one disappointment to another. Stop waiting for your circumstances to change. You are the one who needs to change, and then your circumstances will follow.

Disillusioned with people

The most painful disillusion is the one inflicted upon us by another person. People disappoint us when we expect them to act in a certain way and they do the exact opposite. It could be a friend who fails us when we needed him the most or a boss who plays a dirty trick on us. Sometimes it is a loved one who has been unfaithful to us or the parents we used to honor who have let us down. It could be the politician we trusted who hasn't lived up to our expectations or a pastor who has disappointed us by showing the wrong kind of attitude.

The other day, a young lady from our church told

us about her experience. I believe that it illustrates this point perfectly.

I loved my boyfriend more than anything else in the world because I felt that everybody else had abandoned me. My parents had given me up for adoption so that another family could raise me. I found out about this one day when my adoptive mother, tired of my rebelliousness and bad manners, told me crudely that I wasn't her child and they were not my family. She began to reproach me for all she had done and given to me.

The pain was so intense that I fell into a deep depression. Doctors and psychologists tried to help me, but with no results. I lived in torment and didn't want to talk to anybody. One day I found my mother's sedatives and swallowed them all. A miracle saved my life. I had left a farewell note to my mother, which she found. In desperation, she went to all kinds of healers and witch doctors looking for help.

At that time, my boyfriend was my only source of safety and love. I trusted in him and shared all that was in my heart. One day, he stayed home studying, so I decided to visit a friend who lived close to where he lived. When I got off the bus, I saw my boyfriend hugging and kissing a girlfriend of mine. I couldn't believe my eyes. I didn't even have the strength to get angry. All I felt was an extreme sadness. I returned home. I was tired of things going wrong all the time, and I felt bad that nobody seemed to love me.

It is very painful when people we trust let us down. Our suffering will continue until we realize that we can't put our trust in others. It may seem like an exaggeration, but it really isn't. The psalmist declared, "It is better to take refuge in the LORD than to trust in man. It is better to take refuge in the LORD than to trust in princes" (Ps. 118:8–9). The author of Psalm 146 is even more succinct when he categorically says, "Do not put your trust in princes, in mortal men, who cannot save" (v. 3).

It is important to understand what the Word of God teaches us. It doesn't say that we have to mistrust people totally. We are not to be skeptics who don't believe in anybody, isolating ourselves so that no one gets hurt. Sadly, this is the attitude of many who have been disappointed by people. When the Word tells us not to put our trust in others, it means that our happiness cannot depend on others. Human beings are sinners, and we can't expect much of them—sooner or later, they will let us down. To think any differently is to be ignorant of human nature.

We need to understand that human beings are fallible, and yet we love them anyway. As we keep a realistic understanding of human nature we will not be disappointed when they let us down. Our confidence needs to be in the Lord and in Him alone.

A SURE TRUST

It was a special time for the people of Israel. They were discouraged and disillusioned because their great leader was not going with them into the land to conquer it. So Moses tells them:

> Be strong and courageous, for you must go with this people into the land that the LORD swore to their forefathers to give them, and you must divide it among them as their inheritance. The LORD himself goes before you and will be with you; he will never leave you nor forsake you. Do not be afraid; do not be discouraged.
> —DEUTERONOMY 31:7–8

If you are disillusioned and discouraged right now, you need to know that the Lord is with you and that He is in control. Nothing is outside of His dominion. Your life isn't ruled by chance. Your life is not ruled by your circumstances. If Jesus Christ is your Lord, He is sovereign over every aspect of your life.

With Christ as your Lord, you can face life with the peace and tranquility of knowing that everything is under God's control. Therefore everything will be all right because the God who rules loves us deeply, unconditionally and eternally. His will is always the best for us. He not only wants the best for you, but He also has the power to make it happen, since He is a sovereign God.

The Potter allows disappointment to cleanse us from all deceptive illusions. Sometimes He will allow our dreams to fail so that we can be brought back to reality. When our plans come crashing down, we, as His fragile vessels, accept the Potter's perfect plan for us. Sometimes He will allow others to hurt us so that our trust will be put in Him.

At this time, if you are feeling like an empty vessel, disillusioned and frustrated, I want you to know that the Potter, the God who loves you, wants to fill you with His presence in a very special way. Leave your feelings of failure behind and return to the Potter's house.

Because of all my enemies, I am the utter contempt of my neighbors; I am a dread to my friends—those who see me on the street flee from me. I am forgotten by them as though I were dead; I have become like broken pottery.

—PSALM 31:11–12

5

Broken Jars

JESUS CHRIST SAYS that He came to this world so that we could have life, and have it to the full (John 10:10). When, in His love, the Potter designed us before the foundations of the world, He imagined us living that abundant life. His purpose is that we live from triumph to triumph. Through us He spreads everywhere the fragrance of the knowledge of Him. We are being transformed into His likeness with ever-increasing glory.

Now, if this is true, we need to ask ourselves: Why are there Christians who, instead of living the abundant life, live miserable lives? Why do they go from failure to failure rather than from glory to glory? Why don't they reflect God's glory? Even better, we should ask ourselves: What stops us from living the abundant life, going from triumph to triumph, being transformed with an ever-increasing glory?

I'm convinced that one of the main reasons for this is that there are roots of bitterness in many of us. That bitterness establishes itself in our hearts when life ends up being different than what we had expected. We become full of hatred, resentment, envy and guilt. The result is a disease that takes away our joy in the Lord, prevents us from being transformed by God and slowly destroys us.

At times we feel like David. We have been dishonored. Those who are closest to us and whom we love the most have become our enemies. They have hurt us, left us, abandoned us. We feel that God has forgotten us. We feel as if we were dead. The bitterness that comes from not understanding the reason for our suffering makes us feel like a *broken jar*.

Let us take a close look at the way these roots of bitterness take hold of us and how we can be set free from them.

WHAT IS BITTERNESS?

Bitterness is a subtle poison we drink one sip at a time, which eventually destroys us. As you experience resentment against someone, nothing will happen to that person, but you will be filled with bitterness that will make you spiritually, psychologically and physically sick.

When you are full of envy for the good fortune of others, your heart fills with anger and bitterness, and although those whom you envy are unaffected, you may eventually get sick. The wounds of the past never heal because you continue to open them up again with your thoughts. Memories torture your mind, which is sick with resentment. As a result, your whole life is filled with bitterness.

We have all suffered. Some continue being hurt. I don't intend to say that our pain is imaginary or that the wounds are not there. God wants to heal us. But He will not give us amnesia or erase the bad times from our memory. He will help us to forgive and will heal us, so that when we look back it will not hurt anymore. What has happened to us will remain in the past.

Bitterness is sinister and horrendous. Slowly but surely it will destroy us. Not only that, but it is a contagious disease. Without knowing it, we pass that bitter feeling and taste about life to others. It hurts many and may even destroy a church. It is one of the main barriers to a victorious life and a growing church.

The following story will illustrate my point:

> I was born into a very poor family. My dad was a good man, very hard working, but he drank quite a bit. My mom was a firm authoritarian and very controlling.
>
> From the time I was five or six years old, I noticed a difference between the way my mom

treated my older sisters and the way she treated me. This caused me a lot of pain, and I stored up more and more hatred in my heart. My mother never told me that she loved me; instead, she used to beat me. I used to cry until my eyes were so swollen that I couldn't open them. Even at such a young age, I would ask the Lord why.

When I turned eighteen, I decided to leave home. I went to live in a girls' boarding house. I became alienated, sleeping on benches at train stations or sitting on a bus, going from one place to another, cold and hungry. Every time I had a problem, I would blame my mother for it and hate her even more. But I never told her anything. I kept the resentment in my heart. Some time later, I got married and had two beautiful children. In 1994 I heard you preaching on the radio, and your words touched my heart. I went to King of Kings Church where I accepted the Lord Jesus as my Savior. God started to heal my heart from hatred, anger and resentment. One day as I was praying, I forgave my mom. I cried so much that I made a puddle with my tears. Then I got up, went to her house, hugged her and for the very first time in my life I told her that I loved her.

Today, every time I visit her, I hug her a lot. I never told her anything, never reproached her for what had happened. I know that God broke down the wall that Satan had raised between the two of us. She is now free, and I love her and have peace.

This is the testimony of someone whose life, like a broken jar, was restored by the Potter. Unfortunately there are roots of bitterness in many believers' hearts. We allow our hearts to be filled with bitterness when, as we go through trials and temptations, we rebel instead of recognizing that God knows why He deals with us in that way, and that His will is good, pleasing and perfect. This is the reason why the Word exhorts us:

> See to it that no one misses the grace of God and that no bitter root grows up to cause trouble and defile many.
> —HEBREWS 12:15

HOW CAN WE BE HEALED FROM BITTERNESS?

The first step to healing is to *confess your bitterness* to God. Then *renounce the bitterness—it is a sin.* Stop justifying yourself by saying how much you've suffered because of mistreatment. Don't allow self-pity to rule your life. Repent, and God will justify you. Paul says, "Get rid of all bitterness" (Eph. 4:31).

Pray to the Lord, saying, "Lord, bitterness comes up from my inside and hurts me, yet I don't know what to do. I recognize that You don't like this feeling. I renounce hatred; I renounce this resentment; and I renounce the sin I fall into time after time, which moves me away from You. I renounce my bitterness."

Now *forgive those who have hurt you.* The Bible says, "But if you do not forgive men their sins, your Father will not forgive your sins" (Matt. 6:15). If we are able to forgive others, the Lord will forgive us. Forgive and bless those who have hurt you, who have offended you, rejected you and wounded you.

Allow God to heal you. Receive healing through faith. God will transform all that we deposit into His hands, honestly and confidently. If you allow Him to do so, He will remove the roots of bitterness from your heart.

Finally, *ask for the fullness of the Holy Spirit right now.* The best way to live without bitterness in your heart is to be full of the Holy Spirit.

This testimony will help you to be victorious:

> God has worked in many areas of my life and still does. One of the things that broke my bitterness and deeply touched my heart was being able to forgive a family member whom I had hated and resented for a long time—my father.
>
> His continued arguments, strong character and lack of dialogue filled me with fear, insecurity, pain and sadness. What began as a lack of acceptance, with roots of bitterness, anger and

friction between us, later kept me in bondage, enslaving me.

My life lost all meaning. My body and soul were sick. I felt totally detached from my family, even though I lived with them. My life was like a dark deep pit that held me captive. I experienced loneliness, great fears, feelings of failure, sadness, bitterness and rebelliousness. I was very hurt, and nothing seemed to bring me comfort.

In 1986, the Lord led my mother and sister to King of Kings Church. I started attending the Bible studies and the services also. Something prevented me from praying. I had no peace. There was something I had not surrendered to the Lord—my lack of forgiveness.

I used to pray, "Lord, touch him and change him." But I was the one that had to change. God was going to intervene, but I had to do my part. Through His Word, I could hear Him saying to me, "Do you want to be healed? Do you want to be free?"

The Lord showed me that if I wanted to be forgiven, I had to forgive. If I was asking for mercy, I had to be merciful toward others as well. So I told the Lord, "I don't really feel this, but I want to be free. I choose to forgive out of obedience, out of love for You. Please help me."

Right away, the devil tried to lie to me, saying, "You will never be a Christian; you won't be able to." But God ministered to me in many ways and so, in prayer, I rejected that lie and confessed forgiveness.

I realized that it was just the beginning. I had to step out in faith through action. I started by greeting my dad when he came home, offering him something to drink. It was really hard! I hadn't talked to him in months. I made him a cake and was kind to him as I served dinner. Those were little things, but to me they were great achievements. But the most important thing was still missing. I clearly heard the Holy Spirit's voice saying, "Now love him."

I have to confess, at that point, I thought that my path as a Christian had ended. It was something that seemed impossible for me to do. At that moment God showed me how much He loved me, and how much I had to accept and forgive myself in order to love others.

God started talking to me through His Word, telling me that He had chosen me for a reason, that He knew me from before the foundations of the world, that He had formed me in my mother's womb. He also told me that I was His beloved daughter, special to Him and deeply loved.

All the enemy's strongholds, built throughout the years, fell piece by piece, and lie by lie.

Finally, I was able to understand, through the love of Christ, how much my father had suffered and what he had to go through as a child. Now I could see through the eyes of Jesus and repent for my sin.

Eventually, my father and I became great friends. Now we chat for hours, and every time we meet, we hug and kiss each other. After my decision to forgive, I had peace; before, I couldn't sleep, had emotional problems and relationship problems with other people and physical problems.

I met the God who is "Restorer" and "Healer." He heals even the deepest wounds of the soul, giving us another chance and restoring what the enemy has stolen from us.

Right now, would you like to ask God to cleanse you of all bitterness, resentment, memories and wounds from your past?

> *Lord, I confess my bitterness to You. This is what makes me bitter. (Share your bitterness with the Lord.) I recognize that You don't like my feelings. I renounce the hatred that is poisoning my life and preventing me from growing in You. I renounce the resentment that took hold of me when _____ (be specific). I renounce bitterness. In obedience to You, I remove all bitterness from my heart. I cast it out in the name of Jesus.*

Lord, I forgive those who have hurt me. I forgive _____ (say the name of the person who has hurt you). I bless him/her in the name of Jesus. By faith, Lord, I receive Your healing and the fullness of the Holy Spirit. Amen.

Now, in the name of Jesus, I impart blessing to you and the anointing of restoration. Start to live like a new jar, according to God's plan for your life.

Is this man ... a despised, broken pot, an object no one wants? Why will he and his children be hurled out, cast into a land they do not know?

—JEREMIAH 22:28

6

Despised Jars

THERE ARE TWO powerful images that the Holy Spirit uses to teach us, in a tough but clear way, the reality of failure in the Christian life. I pray that the Lord will reveal to you how serious it is to try to live behind God's back. May this revelation help you to abandon those things that prevent you from enjoying an abundant life.

A DESPISED AND BROKEN JAR: AN UNSUCCESSFUL KING

The first of these images is found in the Book of Jeremiah. The prophet, using very harsh but realistic language, talks about a man whom he compares to a broken and despised jar (Jer. 22:28). Who is this man? Some Bible versions call him Coniah. It was Jehoiachin, king of Judah, a man comparable to a broken and disdained vessel.

Jehoiachin's situation can be useful for prevention or correction, lest God considers our life as a broken and despised jar. Jehoiachin reigned for only three months. In those ninety days, he managed to do evil in the eyes of the Lord (2 Kings 24:9). As a result, God rejected him and condemned him to exile in Babylon, along with his influential mother, Nehushta (v. 8).

The people, seeing their young king in the desert, raised the question found in Jeremiah 22:28. They could not understand the sad fate of their king, now considered, along with his descendants, a broken and despised jar.

Jeremiah overlooks their question and prophesies to the people with these words:

> O land, land, land, hear the word of the LORD! This is what the LORD says: "Record this man as if childless, a man who will not prosper in his lifetime, for none of his offspring will prosper, none will sit on the throne of David or rule anymore in Judah."
>
> —JEREMIAH 22:29–30

God commanded that Jehoiachin's punishment be recorded in history. His rebellion before God caused his descendants to lose all privileges to the throne of David. Because he turned his back on God, he was considered a broken and despised jar.

And the passage tells us even more: "A man who will not prosper in his lifetime." Another version reads: "His life will amount to nothing" (NLT).

Jehoiachin's story is the story of thousands of individuals whose lives are failures. All the books in the world could not contain the record of these kinds of people. The tragedy in Jehoiachin's life is that God had chosen him as king. Only one person in the whole nation of Israel had that possibility. This man destined to be king ended up as a failure, and not only him, but also his offspring. Called to be king by God, he ended as a slave in Babylon.

The Bible says that Jesus Christ "loves us and has freed us from our sins by his blood, and has made us to be a kingdom and priests" (Rev. 1:5–6). How tragic it is to see so many believers who have been made kings by the blood of Jesus Christ, living miserable lives of failure! Created by the Potter to be vessels of honor, yet living ruined lives and ending up as broken and despised jars! Called to be kings, they live like slaves.

A DESPISED AND BROKEN JAR:
A FRUSTRATED CHILDBIRTH

There is nothing more painful in life for a woman than being ready to go into labor, yet knowing that the child she carries is dead. Not only is the baby dead—so are her hopes and dreams.

The Bible uses this painful experience to illustrate a more generalized frustration. It is the frustration experienced by men and women who are never really happy. Life passes them by, and happiness and peace never come. Their general well-being is just a dream for them. This is how the Bible describes it:

> As a woman with child and about to give birth writhes and cries out in her pain, so were we in your presence, O LORD. We were with child, we writhed in pain, but we gave birth to wind.
>
> —ISAIAH 26:17–18

How many of your dreams have given birth to wind? How many desires, conceived in your heart, ended up in nothing? They were not bad dreams, nor were they harmful projects, false aspirations or unjust plans. But they failed and were nothing but wind.

Who doesn't want a solid, happy home? Who doesn't want to be fulfilled in his career? Who hasn't imagined a prosperous, secure future that provides the necessary things to be able to live with dignity? Who doesn't want to be recognized, accepted and respected? Who doesn't long to love and be loved? Is there anything wrong with this? And yet often, as the prophet said, the outcome is that *we gave birth to wind.*

Possibly, in looking back at your life, you feel very much like a woman who has conceived, gone through labor pains, but has given birth to the wind. At each new failure the possibilities of happiness diminish and your heart is filled with bitterness.

If this is your situation, there is hope for you. This is not just silly optimism or an attempt to pass a positive thought on to you so that you don't get discouraged. On the contrary, this hope can become a reality—even today. But you will have to make two basic corrections.

Change your foundation.

Most of our failures are due to building on the wrong foundations. When the results of our plans are bad, it is because the starting point is wrong—our foundations are incorrect, and our basic idea is inaccurate. No matter what our failed dream is, the foundation on which we have intended to build has been to trust in ourselves rather than God.

The businessman who starts his business on a foundation of shady dealings, doing things contrary to God's ways, may prosper, but his end result is clear. He will fail because he is backed by Satan, and he will be held accountable for it.

The person who is in search of a prosperous and secure future without inquiring of God, just trusting in his own intelligence, capacity and strength, will obtain results, but overall well-being will be missing in his life. The young man who starts a relationship on the wrong premises (being unequally yoked, lacking knowledge about the other person, being partial to physical, emotional or spiritual attraction) and doesn't look for God's confirmation is setting himself up for pain, misery, tears and giving birth to wind.

Many believers know that their decisions are not in agreement with God's will, but they still flirt with Satan. Those who do this should expect pain and giving birth to wind. What is God's place in your decisions, relationships and occupations? Whenever God is left out of the picture, all that we reap is failure. We give birth to wind. We become broken and despised vessels.

That is why the prophet urges us to change our foundations. He calls us not to put our trust in our own strength, abilities, intuitions and discernment, but to trust in God: "Trust in the LORD forever, for the LORD, the LORD, is the Rock eternal" (Isa. 26:4). When God is our foundation, we shall not fear. He is our eternal refuge. He is the eternal Rock. We can face all kinds of enemies—circumstances that work against our dreams and try to frustrate our God-given plans, that try to bring down what God is doing in us or in our personal relationships. But if our life is built on the right foundation, on God, neither the circumstances nor our enemies will prevail because God is our eternal refuge. He is the eternal Rock.

You can trust in Jesus. Satan, with all his power, could not defeat Him. He tempted Him, enjoyed His martyrdom and crucifixion and His burial. He was singing victory when his whole body shuddered as he saw that the stone closing the tomb had moved. He was paralyzed in front of the open tomb. He fell on the ground, defeated at Jesus' resurrection. There is no enemy that can prevail against Him. He is our eternal refuge. That is why you need to trust in Him until the end of time. Forever, at all times, in all things, trust in the Lord. He wants to start writing a new life story for you.

Change your orientation.

Many times our dreams, wishes and aspirations fail because we allow those longings to become "lords" of our life.

Many people who try to succeed financially are not just motivated by necessity. They have allowed money to become their god. If we are looking for a spouse, and that need becomes an idol, our happiness or unhappiness will be determined by our success in finding that person. Whatever determines our happiness will eventually become our god. He who seeks recognition or acceptance, and his happiness or unhappiness depends on achieving that goal, has made that his god.

When consciously or unconsciously we let other gods rule us, such as money, family, spouse, status or occupation, we have displaced the one true God. Consequently, we can expect only failure.

The prophet said, "O Lord, our God, other lords

besides you have ruled over us" (Isa. 26:13).

If we do not want to keep on giving birth to wind, Jesus alone must be our Lord. His lordship needs to go from mere theory to practice. You may say along with the prophet: "Other lords ruled my life," but now "they are dead; they live no more; those departed spirits do not rise. We only acknowledge You, God, as the only Lord."

This is the time to repent. The Holy Spirit is breathing His sanctifying anointing over His church. We worship a jealous God. This is the time to renounce our other gods and do it forever. Crucify them; put Jesus Christ in the center, in first place, sitting at the throne of our lives.

What will the outcome be of all of this? The prophet says, "LORD, you establish peace for us; all that we have accomplished you have done for us" (Isa. 26:12). When Christ is our Lord, we can expect Him to give light to a new reality, and not to wind. He makes our dreams and our works come to life. In Him we find victory because He is the eternal Rock.

At age eighteen, failure was Jehoiachin's distinguishing feature. God had called him to be king, and he ended up being a slave. Like thousands of other people in the world and throughout history, he had the feeling of giving birth to wind. Is that all there is in this life? When the Potter thinks about us, is He satisfied to see us as broken and despised jars, old vessels that nobody wants? Of course not! He still has His original design in mind. No one will make Him change the plans He has for us.

He is ready to set His hands on you to reshape you again. But you have to change your foundation and orientation. Depend on Him, and do everything for His glory. The Potter is ready to start to work on you. Don't keep Him waiting!

And every open container without a lid fastened on it will be unclean.

—NUMBERS 19:15

7

Unclean Jars

EXPRESSING IT WITH musical but clear language, someone once said what happens when we sin: "In the eternal harmony, to sin is dissonance." Continuing with the biblical image of the Potter, we realize that when we sin, God's work gets ruined. Let's look at the serious consequences of sin.

In the Book of Leviticus, the Word of God sheds light on this subject through the law regarding leprosy. Leprosy is a symbol of sin. There are interesting parallels that we will consider carefully. Sin, like leprosy, may start small, but it grows and destroys our entire life. Sin, like leprosy, is very contagious. Leprosy desensitizes the person to such an extent that the leper doesn't have any feelings in the affected area. Likewise, when we allow sin in our lives, we can desensitize our conscience and not feel any grief for letting God down.

You may ask, "Pastor Claudio, why are you telling me this?" Because I love you in the Lord, I will be very honest with you. If you sin, the presence of God will not be manifested in your life. If you open the door to any kind of spiritual contamination, it will take away the precious fellowship you share with the Holy Spirit. Therefore, I want you to understand how sin works and what its consequences are. I want you to listen carefully to God's call to a life of holiness.

UNCLEAN JARS ARE OPEN JARS

When we leave our container open, it becomes contaminated and unclean. In the text at the opening of this chapter, it specifically says that the container has to be closed tightly. If not, the container becomes polluted and unclean.

Our Christian lives need to be closed to *Satan's attacks,* to the *world's suggestions* to go against God's will and to the *lust of our own flesh.* If we don't take God's warning seriously and leave our jars open, we are exposed to the enemy's attacks. The devil is like a roaring lion, looking for whom he may devour. The thoughts of this world with its influence and philosophy of life invade our lives and conform us to this polluted world. Our flesh demands to be satisfied, choking and quenching the work of the Holy Spirit.

Paul exhorts us: "Do not give the devil a foothold"

(Eph. 4:27). That means, *close the lid tightly.* Don't leave any space for contamination. Don't have an air of self-sufficiency, but be alert and careful to close your vessel well. "So, if you think you are standing firm, be careful that you don't fall!" (1 Cor. 10:12).

UNCLEAN VESSELS INTERRUPT OUR FELLOWSHIP

Chapter 59 of the Book of Isaiah will help us to understand better the consequences of sin in our lives.

Sin is a rebellious act against God: "Rebellion and treachery against the LORD, turning our backs on our God" (v. 13). Sin prevents us from accepting God's authority over us and prevents Him from being the Lord of our lives. Adam and Eve's sin was to desire to be like God. They didn't want Him to continue ruling and leading them as before. In spite of fully enjoying His communion and experiencing the joy of God's ruling over them, they chose to remove the Lord from their hearts, taking God's place.

Daily we stop God from ruling our lives entirely. We know He is our Potter and Creator, but we don't allow Him to do His work in us. We don't submit to His sovereignty. Instead, we pretend to be the owners of our lives. The Bible calls this sin because we have made the decision to remove God from the center. In our rebelliousness, we have occupied that place ourselves.

The Bible teaches us that God has made a covenant with His children. He promises His care, His blessing, His salvation, His help and His protection on our behalf. Man, on the other hand, has to live according to the rules established by God. These regulations are not capricious or arbitrary, but rather for our good. If we don't obey them, we end up destroying ourselves.

The Bible compares our relationship with God to a marriage. We are the bride of Christ. Every time we transgress His laws, we are being unfaithful to God. James 4:4–5 clearly says, "You adulterous people, don't you know that friendship with the world is hatred toward God? . . . Or do you think Scripture says without reason that the spirit he caused to live in us envies intensely?" In God's eyes, sin is an act of adultery and unfaithfulness to His Holy Spirit.

Yet there is something even worse than this: We also refuse to accept a remedy to eradicate the sin in our lives. God provides a way out of the sin of rebellion and unfaithfulness, but sometimes, instead of accepting it, we reject it.

Sin is an act of rebelliousness and unfaithfulness that worsens when we reject God's solution found in Christ's salvation. Sin separates us from God. As the prophet Isaiah says, "But your iniquities have separated you from your God" (Isa. 59:2). His holiness is perfect and complete. His holiness does not tolerate sin. Sin is a barrier that prevents God from having close fellowship with us and robs us of joy and harmony in our hearts.

No matter how much faith you have, if you haven't repented from your sins—from your rebelliousness and unfaithfulness—it will not be enough to live a victorious Christian life. Sin interrupts your communion with God and must be dealt with.

Many people come to me and say: "Why doesn't God listen to me?" Isaiah himself answers them when he says, "But your iniquities have separated you from your God; your sins have hidden his face from you, so that he will not hear" (Isa. 59:2). Repentance is not an option; it is indispensable, not only to reestablish our relationship with God (the day we receive Jesus Christ into our hearts), but also to cleanse us daily so that we can maintain full communion with Him. When we abandon sin and yield ourselves entirely to Christ, the barrier that separated us is torn down.

Unclean Jars Destroy God's Plans

Sin also prevents us from achieving true satisfaction in life. We are not happy; we don't fill the vacuum inside nor achieve a true realization of our lives, because we have chosen to live apart from God.

We have all we need in Christ, but we can't live God's eternal plan because of our disobedience. The Potter designed your life and created you to be a jar full of happiness, peace, health, forgiveness and light to others. But if we don't allow the artist to shape our lives freely, those ideals that God had in mind when He created us will never get accomplished.

Some people try to find joy in things like money or power, but soon realize that happiness can't be bought. They look for it in certain activities, and all they achieve is tiredness and dissatisfaction. They look for it in noise, but then silence comes, the lights and the sound are turned off and they realize how unhappy they are. Some search for happiness in extramarital sex, but soon get bored of something that God created to be enjoyed in the right context. They look for it by changing spouses as if they were changing a tie or a belt, but they are still unhappy.

Loss of peace is another consequence of our separation from God. We can't enjoy the peace Jesus gives us. Isaiah 59:8 says: "The way of peace they do not know; there is no justice in their paths. They have turned them into crooked roads; no one who walks in them will know peace."

This is the reason why so many believers live in anguish, longing for peace. Not the peace that depends on external circumstances, but the peace that lies in the core of our being and that will remain there forever. Others live enslaved by their fears, and although they look everywhere, they can't find peace. Jesus Christ is the only One who can fill us with real peace if we allow Him to rule in us.

The following story tells of a young woman who was so embittered that she yielded herself to a sinful life. Her story teaches us two things. First, it shows us the terrible consequences of sin. Second, it reveals God's glorious and huge love for us.

I turned off any feelings toward God and those around me. I became religious and practiced Christianity in theory. Three years of coming and going in my relationship with God went by.

Some months later, I met a man who had been a drug addict. He soon became my boyfriend. Both the leaders at church and my parents were against this relationship, but day by day, I continued walking and touching my failure.

This relationship was immersed in lies, strife, insults and disagreements. Trapped by his addiction, my boyfriend left me right before our wedding. I was so crazy as to think that by marrying him, I would not have to endure my father's hatred toward me.

This young man moved to another state, and I fell into a terrible depression. I felt an uncontrollable hatred toward my father. He was opposed to everything I did. I was aware that I had committed many mistakes and let my family down many times, but I felt tortured because my father couldn't forgive me.

Early one morning, feeling abandoned, I

decided to run away from home without telling anybody anything—I just left a note. I felt anger in my heart toward my parents and God. I took all my belongings with me, planning never to come back again. I left thinking that I would find friends, a spouse, work.... But I found only lies, loneliness, hunger, lack of understanding, guilt, disappointment and other unwanted feelings. I started to drink alcohol and to smoke marijuana, and I immersed myself in unfinished love relationships and disappointing friendships.

Soon my life was destroyed. I became anorexic and lost twenty pounds in less than a month.

Some nights I would think about killing myself by throwing myself under a passing train or by taking pills or drugs. But in spite of all this I could sense God's presence following me everywhere I went. He wouldn't leave me alone. I couldn't understand His insistence, since I had openly rejected Him.

One day I just got tired of my depression and of not being able to find a job or a place to live. I couldn't stand the loneliness because, no matter how bad it had been, I was used to living with my family. Drowning in anger, pain and "hunger" for love and acceptance, I called home. I expected yelling and reproaches, but instead I heard my mom's pleading with me to come back home, telling me I was forgiven. And so I did.

But back at home, I didn't go to church and soon abandoned the psychological treatment I was given. I decided to exclude God completely from my life and to remove my father out of my heart forever.

My parents felt morally, socially and spiritually wounded. Time after time they said, "May God's will be done in your life." Threatened by my bursts of anger and my desire to leave again or even to kill myself, they allowed me to sin and to relate to the wrong kind of people.

My father started to punish me verbally. His anger was tremendous and in some ways it was reciprocal. My feelings for him were awful, and yet I hid them, deluding my parents so that I could enjoy some privileges at home.

One day I thought about killing my father with a weapon that he had hidden in the house. I knew where it was, so I took the weapon and caressed it. I wanted to do it without much thinking, but then I quickly put it away.

Thousands of events and countless sinful experiences filled my days. I became involved in criminal activities. It was 1996, and I had started to go to school just to prove that I wasn't good at that either. I continued to sin more and more through night parties, unruly passions, vices and unhappy love affairs. In every situation I would do whatever I wanted to do—but not at home. My father's rules and limitations had me cornered.

I went to a gym that belonged to a young man from King of Kings Church. I could hear them talking about God and listening to Christian music in the place. Instead of leaving, there was something that attracted me to that place, and I started to be concerned about my physical and spiritual condition. I became aware of my own human misery, the hidden things in my life. One afternoon, together with those brothers and sisters, I prayed to the Lord asking for reconciliation, even though I had doubts that I could ever really love Him. I didn't feel anything for Him anymore.

Yet from that moment on God really started to pursue me. He was with me at all times. Even while I was sinning, He was there. I could hear His voice talking to my conscience, telling me that I didn't belong to that world anymore. He would tell me I was His, and that I had never stopped being His in spite of my many rejections. I was troubled by all these feelings, and in my spirit I would contend with Him. He was alluring me with His compassion and His love, and I had no more strength to fight back.

Tired of struggling with God in my thoughts, tired of fighting with my parents, I surrendered to the presence of God in my room. Alone, just Him and me, even though I couldn't see Him or touch Him, I knew He was there. That night we settled all accounts, all the personal issues of my relationship with Him. I was able to cry a lot and receive His comfort and forgiveness. I felt deeply cleansed of all the wrong feelings I had inside. I knew that a very close friendship with the Lord had just started.

Some months went by. Although I continued to sin, I felt God's presence and His pure, clean love, different from any other type of superficial love I had known before.

After reading the book *Holy Spirit, I Hunger for You* by Pastor Claudio Freidzon, I had a wonderful experience with God. I believed that His blood had cleansed me, and I knew that I would never be the same again. I couldn't resist His tremendous love anymore. His love was stronger than all my guilt and my fears.

The Holy Spirit broke insurmountable spiritual and psychological strongholds that had been inside of me for years. I felt a special kind of love for my father. I had never loved him like this before, and I couldn't wait for the next day to come, when I would tell him how much I loved him. A wonderful restoration started to take place.

One evening, while doing some silly chore, I started to cry. It didn't make sense, but suddenly I was filled with the love and the forgiveness of

God. Crying, I approached my dad and asked him if we could talk. I asked his forgiveness for all the hatred that I had felt for him for all those years. Likewise, he asked for my forgiveness for not having known how to deal with me correctly. We talked peacefully and confessed all the hurt we had inflicted on each other. We agreed to nurture the new father-daughter relationship that was developing that night. We prayed together and asked God to teach us both to be kind and respectful in spite of our flaws.

Currently I attend King of Kings Church in Belgrano and also the discipleship groups. I feel loved and respected by my brothers and sisters in the faith. Now I can understand that this is much more than a religion; it is a deep love relationship of daily commitment. Every day I decide to love Him more, and that helps me to love my dad, in spite of his faults.

God started a new work in me and will be faithful to complete it. I believe that He will use my life as a vessel to talk to those who are hurting, who need God's true love and compassion for their broken lives, torn by life's circumstances.

What a good and merciful God we have! It is beautiful to see this young lady today, so full of love and the purity of Christ.

Let's take a look at some other consequences of sin. *Sickness* is one consequence. Isaiah 59:10 says, "Among the strong, we are like the dead." How many believers are constantly sick? They go to see their doctor, and he tells them that they are all right. Yet they feel sick. The psalmist experienced this when he said, "When I kept silent, my bones wasted away through my groaning all day long" (Ps. 32:3).

Another consequence is *guilt: Our sins accuse us.* These are believers whose conscience and guilty feelings rob them of peace. They are tormented by the devil, the accuser. They have the power that raised Jesus from the dead, but it is a dormant power, in captivity, because of sin.

Another consequence suffered by believers when they turn their backs to God, is that they *walk in darkness.* "We look for light, but all is darkness; for brightness, but we walk in deep shadows. Like the blind we grope along the wall, feeling our way like men without eyes. At midday we stumble as if it were twilight" (Isa. 59:9–10). The Christian who, knowing the light, chooses to live outside the will of God, will walk like that. He is like the blind. God can't use him to serve and bless others, because it would be like the story of the blind woman standing on the sidewalk waiting for someone to help her cross the street. Suddenly, a man came by and said, "May I go with you to the other side of the street?

"Oh, yes, I would be delighted," she answered.

He held her hand, and they started to cross the street. About halfway across, he tripped. So the woman said, "What is going on? You walk like a blind man."

"I am blind," he answered. "That is why I asked you if we could cross the street together."

God is not only annoyed with our sin, He is also displeased that we don't fully live the abundant life He prepared for us and that Jesus gained for us on the cross. Isaiah 59:16 says, "He saw that there was no one, he was appalled that there was no one to intervene; so his own arm worked salvation for him, and his own righteousness sustained him." He has sent the Redeemer, the Liberator to make a covenant with those who repent. We need to repent and be forgiven. The apostle John teaches us, "If we claim to have fellowship with him yet walk in the darkness, we lie and do not live by the truth" (1 John 1:6). We have to reestablish our intimate and daily communion with Him.

When we sin, we don't stop being God's children, but our communion with Him is interrupted. The conscience is now affected. And when our conscience is unclean, our fellowship with Him is broken.

UNCLEAN JARS ARE BROKEN

What happens when we repeat the same sins constantly and reluctantly turn our backs to God's will?

100

The time comes when God establishes His discipline. David experienced this after committing sin with Bathsheba. God's discipline fell on him: "For day and night your hand was heavy upon me; my strength was sapped as in the heat of the summer" (Ps. 32:4).

If we confess our sins sincerely, we will be forgiven and our communion with God will be instantly restored. However, God may change His way of dealing with us and discipline us for our benefit. If the discipline is accepted, then it fulfills its task and correction is received. God then lifts the discipline. But, this may take a long time.

The Book of Leviticus says, "If one of them falls into a clay pot, everything in it will be unclean, and you must break the pot" (Lev. 11:33). His hand is heavy and tough, but loving. When His hand of discipline falls on us, there is brokenness. The jar breaks. With reality, the author of the Book of Hebrews says, "No discipline seems pleasant at the time, but painful. Later on, however, it produces a harvest of righteousness and peace for those who have been trained by it" (Heb. 12:11).

If we confess every sin we commit with sincerity of heart, they will be pardoned. Fellowship is restored instantly, but we still may have to endure a time of discipline. Therefore, from the very beginning of our Christian life we have to obey God seriously, so that He doesn't have to discipline us.

Cover your life and tighten the lid so that the devil

does not have an entry point. Then God will not have to discipline you. If you are undergoing discipline and are like a broken jar, turn to God with all humility and accept the way He is dealing with you. In due time the Potter will restore you and give you a new chance. God will make you into a new jar according to His perfect design.

You turn things upside down, as if the potter were thought to be like the clay! Shall what is formed say to him who formed it, "He did not make me"? Can the pot say of the potter, "He knows nothing"?

—Isaiah 29:16

8

Rebellious Jars

GOD SPOKE THROUGH the prophet Isaiah to a rebellious and proud people to show them the arrogance, blindness and hypocrisy existing among them. But the people, rather then recognizing their situation, became even more proud and considered themselves wise and knowledgeable. Thus, God had to rebuke them, and tells them that no matter how wise and learned they thought they were, because of their depravity and pride they were nothing but clay. He demonstrated how they were making fools of themselves by rebelling against their Creator. Certainly it was a ridiculous and grotesque attitude.

Pride puts us in a similar situation today. Whenever we sin, we tend to blame somebody or something else. If it is not our mother-in-law, it will be our spouse, our children, our circumstances, the country, the pastor, the president, Satan or someone else. This is the way to transfer our responsibility unto others. We all like to do this.

Some time later we realize that this becomes a vicious cycle, a boomerang that ends up hitting us. We generate an environment where no one takes responsibility for his or her own mistakes and is constantly blaming others. And so we end up getting blamed for other people's faults.

Elijah ministered as a prophet during King Ahab's reign. Ahab was a king who, according to what the Bible tells us, "did more evil in the eyes of the LORD than any of those before him" (1 Kings 16:30). Ahab's tragedy was not the result of sheer chance. It was the consequence of a sin that characterized not only his life, but the life of the entire nation and his forefathers.

His sin was the original sin—pride. It is original, but it is not unique. On the contrary, it is the most common of all sins. It is original because it originates all other sins. Pride is responsible for all our evils. It is the root of our other sins. We can blame it for everything. But even though pride is the root of all evil, we are responsible for it.

THE CONSEQUENCES OF PRIDE

First Kings 16:21–34 talks about four different consequences of pride.

Pride produces division.

In verse 21, we read that a struggle for power had divided the people in two: "Then the people of Israel were split into two factions; half supported Tibni son of Ginath for king, and the other half supported Omri."

You don't have to be a genius to realize that behind this struggle for power was pride. The power issue had nothing to do with serving the people. It was the vehicle to satisfy their ambition and personal pride.

This could also happen in churches. God's people divide because of their pride. This happened in the church at Corinth. Some followed Paul, others Apollos and others Cephas. Each group proudly professed that they were the only ones following Jesus. (See 1 Corinthians 1:12.) Today we need to pray for unity in the body of Christ and to avoid any denominational friction so that the world will see that we are one.

Another form of pride that leads to division is gossip. We criticize others as a subconscious effort to feel superior to them. This brings division to the church. There may be no other sin as damaging to the church as pride disguised as gossip. Gossip is a cancer within the church that kills it. The church needs to defend itself against this enemy that intends to bring division to the body.

The best way to do this is by reporting gossip. If a

thief or a murderer breaks into your house, you would not hesitate to report him to the police. Well, likewise, when the church-killer, the one who gossips, breaks in, he needs to be reported, too.

If your church is a congregation that wishes to live in the center of God's will and is open to the ongoing renewal of the Holy Spirit, allow me to tell you that its name will be constantly on everybody's lips. It will be the target of many who, due to their frustration, don't have anything better to do than criticize others. Whenever we are at the forefront, we'll get hit. Nevertheless, be humble and never cease to bless them and love them as Jesus taught us to do.

For the forefront to advance, it needs its rear guard covered. Your church cannot afford to be divided. Lack of unity produces defeat. We are challenged to make every effort to keep the unity of the Spirit through the bond of peace.

Pride leads to failure.

All we know about Omri is that he did evil in the eyes of the Lord and sinned more than all those before him. (See 1 Kings 16:25.) Nice summary, right? We are also told that the other events of his reign and the things he achieved are written in the book of the annals of the kings of Israel (1 Kings 16:27). This book is not one of the books in our Bible. In the eyes of God, Omri had an undistinguished life. The record of his achievements is found only in the archeological records that seem to indicate that he had fame and success. In fact, for an entire century the Assyrians called Israel *"the house of Omri."*

Omri ended up being someone important in the eyes of the world. His constructions were notorious, but they were the fruit of pride. But the humble have their story recorded in the Word of God and are used by Him to change history and impact the world.

In His time, Jesus died as a perfect stranger to the world around Him. And yet, history today is divided into two periods: before and after Christ. None of the secular historians in the primitive world spoke about Peter or John or any of the other apostles. However, those few illiterate men revolutionized the Roman Empire.

The story of God's people will always be the story of a people without history. And yet, they are the people who alter the history of the world. Because they make room for God to work, the humble change the world. They do not trust in their own strength or intelligence; they allow the work of God to become a reality.

That is why the Bible says that God chose the foolish, the weak, the despicable and the despised things of the world to shame the wise.

Pride prevents God from working. The power of God is perfected in weakness. When there is humility, God does the work and changes history.

Truly, Omri stood out in his time and was powerful and famous. But all we know today is that he was one of the worst kings of Israel. That is his reputation.

If your attitude is correct, it really doesn't matter whether you are rich or poor, whether you have material, emotional or physical needs or not. The important thing is that God has you in His sight. He wants to perfect His power in your weakness.

When I graduated from seminary, I had the typical "I-can-do-anything" attitude of many young men. I used to say, "I will preach the gospel," thinking that the theological and pastoral knowledge I had acquired in seminary would be sufficient to have a fruitful ministry. In those days, a dear brother who was an Assemblies of God missionary offered to help me buy some property and open up a church in a beautiful neighborhood with pretty houses and circular streets in the City of Buenos Aires, called Parque Chás.

When we arrived at the place, right across the street from the property we had just bought was a park full of children and young people, so we started to plan an evangelistic crusade. In my enthusiasm, I told Betty, "In two or three months we'll turn the neighborhood upside down."

It was 1979, and the country was pretty closed to the gospel, but I thought we could do it. We placed some chairs in the park and started to preach. Soon my dreams came crashing down. Not one person

It coul
examp
and re
what h
a sin,
backs
us, sin
Adam
is a wa
from o
   Pride
God, r
giving
Him fr
that, a
workin
going g
In the
This is
that se
produc
sion, si
which v
to "stoj
root of
us away

Pride g
   A ve

came near to listen to us. Day after day the chairs remained empty.

Then someone suggested the following: "Why don't you show movies?" We thought that was actually a good idea, and so this time we were able to capture the neighbors' attention. Some very old ladies came and sat in the first row. A few more neighbors were watching with interest. This encouraged us. They were beautiful movies, and after we were done showing them we had an opportunity to preach. Excited and with the Bible in my hand, I was waiting for the big moment to come.

The movie ended, and when we turned the lights on…surprise! They all ran away except for the poor old ladies who didn't have the physical strength to do that! I felt really frustrated.

I looked for alternatives. We would not give up. After examining the situation with my wife, we decided that once the movie ended, I needed to climb up the platform faster. So we rehearsed our plan at home. I would hide behind a tree holding the microphone. As soon as the movie ended my wife would turn on the lights, and I would jump as fast as I could onto the platform to preach a powerful message!

Many people came that next evening. I was in position with the microphone in my hand. The moment the light went on, I jumped to the platform and said in a very loud voice, "Don't go! I have good news for you."

Ahab's time, Hiel of Bethel rebuilt Jericho. He laid its foundations at the cost of his firstborn son Abiram, and he set up its gates at the cost of his youngest son Segub, in accordance with the word of the LORD spoken by Joshua son of Nun" (1 Kings 16:34).

In order to understand this clearly, we have to read Joshua 6:26:

> At that time Joshua pronounced this solemn oath: "Cursed before the LORD is the man who undertakes to rebuild this city, Jericho: At the cost of his firstborn son will he lay its foundations; at the cost of his youngest will he set up its gates."

God cannot be mocked. God judges and punishes our pride and our lack of dependence on Him. Christians who don't deny themselves daily are frustrated and continually fail. That is why there are so many embittered Christians. Pride and self-sufficiency have a sure result—punishment.

When we have the wrong orientation, the punishment will not be momentary, but permanent: a bitter existence here in this world and eternal punishment in the world to come.

Jesus did not come to condemn the world, but to save it. And the way to do it, in His own words, is: "If anyone would come after me, he must deny himself and take up his cross daily and follow me"

(Luke 9:23). To deny oneself means to renounce basic pride. To take up the cross means to renounce daily pride. And to follow Him is to allow Him to rule our lives.

This is the time for the Potter to change your story as a rebellious jar. He wants to change you into the design He has for you. He wants to change your life story, so that you can change the history of this world and these times through the gospel of Jesus Christ. Don't resist Him; let Him mold you!

Then he shall take some holy water in a clay jar and put some dust from the tabernacle floor into the water.

—Numbers 5:17

9

Jars of Curse

IN ANCIENT ISRAEL, there was a very peculiar
ceremony that reflected an old practice established
in the Mosaic Law. Its purpose was to determine the
guilt or innocence of a person suspected of adultery.
The Book of Leviticus would sentence the adulterous
person to death. When there were not enough proofs
for the wife's guilt or innocence to be demonstrated,
the husband had to bring her to the priest, together
with an offering called *the offering for jealousy*. The
priest would take some holy water in a clay jar and
some dust from the tabernacle floor, which he would
put it into the water. The holy water, contaminated
by the dust, would turn into bitter water that brings
a curse. The woman had to drink that water, and if
she had committed the sin of adultery, she would
come under the curse, her abdomen would swell
and she would be barren forever. This was a horrible

punishment in a society that gave tremendous importance to having many children.

Apart from the peculiarity of this ritual, there is a great lesson for us to learn. The jar of clay is our life, and God has destined it to contain holy water. However, when we are unfaithful to God, the dust of sin pollutes it, and we stop being a jar holding holy water and become a jar holding bitter water that brings a curse.

Just as *unfaithfulness* means "to lead a dual relationship," likewise *spiritual adultery* is to say that we love God and are His children while living in disobedience to Him. The dual Christian believes that he can walk two different paths at the same time. He wants to live in two worlds. He doesn't make up his mind. He is a jar containing holy water—but also dust. He ends up being a jar of curse.

THE DIVIDED HEART

Some Christians lead a double life. They enjoy God's presence in meetings; they touch His glory, but in their own private lives they lead a different existence. Their lives look like the description given by the prophet Haggai, who said, "Now this is what the LORD Almighty says: 'Give careful thought to your ways. You have planted much, but have harvested little. You eat, but never have enough. You drink, but never have your fill. You put on clothes, but are not warm. You earn wages, only to put them in a purse with holes in it'" (Hag. 1:5–6).

Such believers have joy, holiness and fellowship while they are in church. But as soon as they get back home, everything changes. They experience loneliness, sadness, spiritual emptiness and strife. From a climate of glory they go into a different spiritual atmosphere. Do they perhaps lose the anointing on the way? Certainly we have to reflect on this.

The apostle Peter admonishes us, "Be self-controlled and alert. Your enemy the devil prowls around like a roaring lion looking for someone to devour" (1 Pet. 5:8). Satan attacks the believers' lives in order to divide their soul: "Or they will tear me like a lion and rip me to pieces with no one to rescue me" (Ps. 7:2). Satan, as a lion, attacks our soul to rip it apart and divide it. James tells us to submit to the lordship of Christ and to resist the devil in order to prevent our soul from being divided: "Submit yourselves, then, to God. Resist the devil, and he will flee from you. Come near to God and he will come near to you. Wash your hands, you sinners, and purify your hearts, you double-minded" (James 4:7–8).

The word James uses is *dypsikos,* which literally means "two souls, two minds and two hearts." According to the Bible, Satan's objective, when he divides, is to destroy: "Every kingdom divided against itself will be ruined, and every city or household divided against itself will not stand" (Matt. 12:25).

Satan knows that as long as our heart is divided, we will not be able to love God with all our soul. What is it that God asks of us in His Word? "And now, O Israel, what does the LORD your God ask of you but to fear the LORD your God, to walk in all his ways, to love him, to serve the LORD your God with all your heart and with all your soul, and to observe the LORD's commands and decrees that I am giving you today for your own good?" (Deut. 10:12–13).

Our divided soul attempts to serve two masters. But as Jesus taught us, this is impossible: "No one can serve two masters. Either he will hate the one and love the other, or he will be devoted to the one and despise the other. You cannot serve both God and Money" (Matt. 6:24). Jesus gives us the example of someone who serves two masters. The result will be that he will love one and despise the other, since it is impossible to serve two masters with absolute and exclusive love. We can't be under the lordship of Christ and at the same time do whatever we want to do. Proverbs clearly declares, "The way of the LORD is a refuge for the righteous, but it is the ruin of those who do evil" (Prov. 10:29). The way of the Lord is a stronghold for the believer who is "whole"—authentic and consecrated. But he who pretends to live his Christian life "divided"—following his own will and doing whatever he wants to do—will end up in destruction.

Not too long ago, I received a letter from a man

telling me about his terrible experience. He was a drug addict and an alcoholic. As expected in a case like his, his family was destroyed. His wrong behavior enormously affected his wife and children. Since his addictions and emotional imbalance would not allow him to work, he would steal in order to be able to provide food for his family.

One day he stopped one of the many taxicabs in the city of Buenos Aires with the intention of robbing its driver. He got in and gave a random address to the driver. A few blocks later, he pulled a gun. He told the man to give him all the money. To his surprise, the driver, who was a member of our church, turned around, looked him in the eyes and said, "Jesus loves you!"

This man told me that it was as if lightning ran through his body. He had been a Christian before, but was now far away from God. He had been part of a church, but then he left and started to live in sin. He even got involved in "spiritism" and a sect called "umbanda." That is the reason why those words coming from a man full of the Holy Spirit moved him so much.

His first reaction was to step down and run away, but our brother would not let him. He grabbed his hand and said, "Don't go! You have to listen to the Word of God. You are stealing because you need Jesus Christ in your life." They talked for a long time, and later this man rededicated his life to the

Lord. After praying together, our brother took him home and bade him good-bye, promising to come by to pick him up to go to church the following Sunday.

That is how he got connected with us and soon after, he wrote us his beautiful letter. I need to share with you an important piece of information about this letter. Do you know where he was when he wrote me? *He was in jail.* God had given him a wonderful opportunity, but he ended up worse than before. He is a clear example of the consequences of having a divided heart.

God doesn't appreciate the dual Christian, and people don't either. They will only respect those who are coherent and truly committed to their beliefs. Even when they don't agree with a person's beliefs, they will show respect. It is easy to see this among teenagers. Those who do things halfheartedly get mocked; on the contrary, those who are committed, live a consistent life and have a wonderful joyous attitude, are not. If teenagers perceive that a committed believer is inclined to help and give good counseling, they will support him. At the time of need, he will be the one to whom they go, since they notice that he is different. When they observe a consistency between what a person believes and what he does, they will offer respect and even admiration. The Book of Deuteronomy explains it this way: "Observe them [God's decrees and laws] carefully, for this will show your wisdom and understanding to the nations, who will hear about all these decrees and say, 'Surely this great nation is a wise and understanding people'" (Deut. 4:6).

People reject those who are inconsistent and whose faith and behavior diverge. They have an external rather than an internal faith: "You are always on their lips but far from their hearts" (Jer. 12:2). They know the Word of God, make gestures like the rest, pray and sing. God is always on their lips but not on the throne of their hearts, ruling their existence. They believe that it is all right to be a Christian in some areas of their lives, but not in others; they think that they are free to choose in what things or aspects of their lives they will obey God and do His will. They don't understand the command that says, "In all your ways acknowledge him, and he will make your paths straight" (Prov. 3:6).

For some believers, it is normal to live a dual life. But I would like us to understand what that means to God. He is angry with the divided believer: "For forty years I was angry with that generation; I said, 'They are a people whose hearts go astray, and they have not known my ways'" (Ps. 95:10). God also declared, "So I declared on oath in my anger, 'They shall never enter my rest'" (v.11). It is not a joke. God takes duality very seriously and says that the person who lives that way is guilty: "Their heart is deceitful [is divided], and now they must bear their guilt" (Hos. 10:2).

God wants Christians to be whole, not divided. He

wants men and women who love Him with all their heart, with all their soul and with all their strength. He is waiting for us to decide: "See, I am setting before you the way of life and the way of death" (Jer. 21:8). This is the time to choose which way to go.

THE NEED TO DECIDE

The people of Israel worshiped God. That wasn't the problem. The real problem was that they also worshiped Baal: "Even while these people were worshiping the LORD, they were serving their idols. To this day their children and grandchildren continue to do as their fathers did" (2 Kings 17:41). The prophet Hosea had to report that this people had a divided heart: "Their heart is deceitful" (Hos. 10:2). This has been Israel's endless problem.

James instructs us saying that "a double-minded man [is] unstable in all he does" (James 1:8). This is many Christians' problem today. They go to church and worship God, but parallel to that, they worship other very subtle gods—money, jobs, family, social standing and their vocation. There's nothing wrong with these things, but when they come first in a person's life, when they determine their happiness or sadness, their peace or their lack of peace, then they become gods that usurp the place of our God.

In the Sermon on the Mount, Jesus told His listeners to make up their minds. They couldn't serve both God and mammon, the god of money. Many Christians want to serve God while constantly focusing on making money. There is nothing wrong with making money, but when it becomes the center of our lives, then it becomes, consciously or unconsciously, an idol.

Mammon is a shrewd god that penetrates and operates in people's hearts. The only one that operates out of grace, that is, at no cost at all, is God. False gods will always charge a fee. Generally they will exchange one thing for another. Mammon will give you things, but in exchange it will require your heart. That is the reason why Jesus taught us that "where your treasure is, there your heart will be also" (Matt. 6:21). Mammon offers you the whole world in exchange for your heart. Consequently, Jesus clearly admonished us, "What good will it be for a man if he gains the whole world, yet forfeits his soul? Or what can a man give in exchange for his soul?" (Matt. 16:26).

I am not against prosperity. My family, my church and I are living testimonies of a God who greatly prospers us. What I'm trying to say is that it is important to discern from where the prosperity is coming. The devil is a clever imitator of God's blessings. The reason for his imitations is so that he can entrap believers. They think God is blessing them, while in reality they are slowly walking away from Him.

Satan applies the principle of "divide and conquer." He knows that if he succeeds in dividing our heart, he will be able to rule our lives, since we will no longer be under God's lordship and will. He never tries to seduce us by saying, "Divide your heart; worship God *and* me." He knows the believer would immediately reject that kind of invitation. So he uses a cleverly disguised bait with a sharp hook hidden inside. He presents good things to us; eventually, those good things will take God's place in our lives, thus becoming idols.

So money and riches could be the bait for some people. But for others, the bait might be family. Some become obsessed with their family and live just for them. Since they need to devote themselves to their family, they never seem to have any time to work for God's kingdom. So Jesus, the Creator and loving sustainer of the family, had to say: "If anyone comes to me and does not hate his father and mother, his wife and children, his brothers and sisters—yes, even his own life—he cannot be my disciple" (Luke 14:26). Obviously, Jesus is not teaching us to hate our parents or children or brothers and sisters or any other relative. What He is saying is that anyone loving a relative more than God can't be His disciple. The essence of following Jesus Christ is that He needs to be first in our lives, our families will be second and our ministry and Christian service will be third.

I have shown you how Satan can divide your heart using money and family as baits. The same could be said of work, your profession, sex, your home, a sport or any other thing that occupies first place in your life. Even church and ministry, if they take God's place, can become false gods. When we are entrapped by these idols, we are in bondage to demons. When a person lives for something and that something becomes his god, and the best of his efforts, motivations and energies are laid on the altar of that god, he is actually sacrificing his life to idols. The Bible says that sacrifices to idols "are offered to demons, not to God, and I do not want you to be participants with demons" (1 Cor. 10:20).

Some believers, although they have experienced God, received precious gifts and talents and possess His anointing, still do not surrender completely to Him. They are divided, and their hearts are divided, too. According to James, they need to be purified: "Wash your hands, you sinners, and purify your hearts, you double-minded" (James 4:8).

A group of young people from our church were deeply touched by God during a time of prayer. They felt the need to consecrate entirely their hearts and leave behind those little gods that clouded God's vision for their lives. One young woman said:

> The Lord is asking me to abandon my selfishness, those things that are important to me, to become involved in the things that are important to Him, the things that are in His heart. We

are not our own, but we are Christ's servants. We are in this world to do His will, to obey and serve Him.

Another young lady testified:

When we prayed, when we were seeking God, I realized that I was taking care of my own business, of my own goals. I wasn't aware of all the people around me in need of the gospel. They are God's opportunity for me to preach the Good News, and I should not waste it.

These are the testimonies of purified hearts. They are hearts lined up with God's will. Do you think God wants to do the same with you?

In a very particular period in Israel's history, again the people's hearts were divided. A confrontation arose between Elijah and the God of Israel and Baal and the prophets of Jezebel. Elijah confronted them with a question that still prevails for us today: "How long will you waver between two opinions?" (1 Kings 18:21). The people worshiped the Lord, but also Baal. That was an abomination for God. Therefore, the anointed prophet had to shake them with this question. The Amplified Bible reads, "How long will you halt and limp between two opinions?" God doesn't like us to play games with Him, so He is asking you today, "How long?"

Longing for a response, the prophets of Baal invoked their god from morning till noon. But nothing—no voice; no answer. They danced around the altar they had made, but nothing. They shouted and cried out, but nothing. They slashed themselves with swords and spears until their blood flowed, but nothing. Midday passed, and they continued their frantic shouting until the time for the sacrifice, but there was no voice, no response; no one answered. Our little gods can satisfy us for a while, but in the crucial times, they are no good. They don't listen to us, and they don't respond. There is only one true God who can listen to our prayers and satisfy our lives.

The Word says that the people said nothing when Elijah confronted them with the question, "How long will you waver between two opinions?" "But the people said nothing." There is nothing that bothers God more than the silence of the undecided, of those who won't make a decision. With very harsh language, the Lord warns us, "I know your deeds, that you are neither cold nor hot. I wish you were either one or the other! So, because you are lukewarm—neither hot nor cold—I am about to spit you out of my mouth" (Rev. 3:15–16). God prefers the cold to the lukewarm. The cold will have the end they freely chose. But woe to the lukewarm man! He thinks he belongs to God, but God will spit him out of His mouth. The cold can repent, but the lukewarm don't even know they need to.

Yet this is a time of restoration. That is why we have to be aware of the seriousness of living a double life. We have to become whole and change our divided heart into one heart. To do this *we must first return to Him:* "And when you and your children *return* to the LORD your God and obey him with *all* your heart and with *all* your soul..." (Deut. 30:2, emphasis added). Many experience only a partial conversion and never experience a victorious Christian life. Today, God calls us to a radical, complete, whole-life conversion.

We have to love the Lord with all that is within us: "And now, O Israel, what does the LORD your God ask of you but to fear the LORD your God, to walk in all his ways, to *love* him, to serve the LORD with *all* your heart and with *all* your soul" (Deut. 10:12, emphasis added). The Lord should be our first and greatest love. No other love can occupy His place.

We have to obey Him completely: "The LORD your God commands you this day to *follow* these decrees and laws; carefully observe them with *all* your heart and with *all* your soul" (Deut. 26:16, emphasis added). The love God requires of us is not a sentimental love. It is a true love that is demonstrated by our inclination to obedience. Jesus understood this when He said, "If you love me, you will obey what I command" (John 14:15).

We have to serve the Lord with our whole being: "But be very careful to keep the commandment and the law that Moses the servant of the LORD gave you: to love the LORD your God, to walk in all his ways, to obey his commands, to hold fast to him and to serve him with *all* your heart and *all* your soul" (Josh. 22:5, emphasis added). "Now fear the LORD and *serve* him with all *faithfulness*. Throw away the gods your forefathers worshiped beyond the River and in Egypt, and *serve* the LORD" (Josh. 24:14, emphasis added).

We have to walk faithfully. Besides being a moment of decision and conversion, the Christian life is about walking faithfully and truthfully: "And that the LORD may keep his promise to me: 'If your descendants watch how they live, and if they *walk faithfully* before me with *all* their heart and soul, you will never fail to have a man on the throne of Israel'" (1 Kings 2:4, emphasis added).

We have to seek Him intensely every day. We must hunger and thirst after God, truly seeking Him, wanting more and more of Him. "They entered into a covenant to *seek* the LORD, the God of their fathers, with *all* their heart and soul" (2 Chron. 15:12, emphasis added).

We have to promise God that He will be our only God. He must know that we will love Him, obey Him, serve Him, seek Him and follow Him forever: "The king stood by the pillar and renewed the

131

covenant in the presence of the LORD—to follow the LORD and keep his commands, regulations and decrees with *all* his heart and *all* his soul, and to obey the words of the covenant written in this book" (2 Chron. 34:31, emphasis added).

The Potter promises that if we truly seek Him, He will put an end to our double life, our double heart and our double path. "I will give them singleness of heart and action, so that they will always fear me for their own good and the good of their children after them" (Jer. 32:39). If this is the way we choose to live from now on, the Potter will restore our life, and we won't be vessels of curse any longer. We will not hold bitter waters anymore, but holy ones.

But the pot he was shaping from the clay was marred in his hands.

—JEREMIAH 18:4

1 0

Hardened Jars

JEREMIAH WAS DISCOURAGED. His heart was torn at the reality of a defeated people heading into destruction. And yet, God didn't leave him sunk in his depression, but instead told him to go down to the potter's house. There he saw the artist at work. He watched him take the clay into his hands and put it on the wheel. He was surprised when he saw that with a simple touch of the potter's fingers, a jar started to take shape. But when it all seemed to be finished...the jar was marred in his hands! However the potter, unmoved, picked up the broken vessel's clay and mixed it again and put it back on the wheel. Soon after, a beautiful new jar was molded.

THE REALITY OF YOUR FAILURE

From the day you were born, God picked you up and

put you on the wheel where He has been molding you for many years. Possibly, you have some cracks and have become a piece of broken jar. You have failed, and on the floor lie the pieces of the man or woman you could have been according to God's plans. What will God do? He created you with a purpose that is still unfulfilled. Will He grab another person to fulfill your purpose? Will He choose someone else to do the work He had designed for you to do? Maybe yes. But perhaps, as we saw in the first chapter, not yet.

Instead of grabbing another piece of clay to shape the jar He had planned, He returns and looks for you. His hand goes over thousands, millions until He finds you. He wants to pick up the fragments and start all over again.

It is very important to understand that He is the God of second chances. Accept your frustration and try to understand the reason why you've failed. Otherwise, you will repeat the same old story again. Coming to terms with our reality is the beginning of our restoration. It is pointless to try to hide the truth, because in the depth of your being there is that bitter taste of failure. Therein lies that longing for the holiness that you can never achieve in your life, and a desire for victory in your Christian life.

Did the jar break because of the potter's lack of skill? Did God fail? Isaiah helps us answer that question when he says, "You turn things upside down, as if the potter were thought to be like the clay! Shall what is formed say to him who formed it, 'He did not make me'? Can the pot say of the potter, 'He knows nothing'?" (Isa. 29:16).

When a child is born, the parents imagine the best future possible for that baby. Likewise, God has imagined the best for you. You are not a mistake! He chose you just as you are. Not wiser, richer, prettier or more important.

For a moment, let's imagine what took place. The potter puts the clay on the wheel and starts to shape it. Everything goes well until he reaches a certain place, a crack, an imperfection that resists his work. He continues shaping the clay, but with every round of the wheel, he faces the thing that prevents him from finishing his work in a satisfactory manner. What is the problem? Is it the potter? His mind and artistic abilities are intact. His capacity to mold is the same. The problem is the resistance on the part of the clay.

THE REASON FOR OUR FAILURE

As Evelyn Christenson says, "There is a place in which we resist God's will. It is the place of our failure." We try to forget about it, but the Holy Spirit keeps on reminding us and bringing it to mind. That is the point, the place where my will is stuck. It is that space in my life where I like to be in control without allowing God to rule.

But when we prostrate ourselves before Him and forever surrender to His will, then the Potter takes us and molds us into beautiful jars. Jacob went to the Potter's house, and the Lord transformed this cheater into a servant, an Israel, a prince of God. Peter went to the same house, and he bitterly cried, humbling himself before God. Later he would go through Pentecost. God's methods have not changed. He wants to do the same thing with you. Does your life taste bitter? Did frustration leave a mark in your life? Are you possibly resisting instead of surrendering?

Lack of forgiveness is a point of resistance that frustrates God's plans. How many Christians resist the Potter in this area! Many have to lose everything before they finally figure out the reason for their failure. The Potter will bring any impurity that prevents His work to light—even those you didn't know existed. The story of a young man in our ministry is a good example of the way God works:

In mid-1990, God dealt with me deeply. At that time, I was leading a group of teenagers every Monday at our church.

I phoned one of the young men in my group because God had laid a burden on me, and I had a feeling that something was wrong with him. His parents had been separated for ten years, and he had not been able to get over it. In spite of living with his mother and her new partner, the wound remained opened. The pain increased that Monday when he heard his mom on the phone with a new "friend," which confirmed that those sweet glances between the two of them were the cause of her pulling away from his "second dad." We agreed to meet early in church to talk.

He was drowning in his tears, and it was hard for me to be firm in my words telling him to forgive. We cried together as we asked God to teach him to love and to forgive. We gave thanks, and we worshiped Him.

Evening came and the presence of the Holy Spirit was covering us with His peace. The church started to fill up with young people. The topic that evening was forgiveness. We said farewell, and I went home with my wife. It was Monday...but it would not be just another Monday.

After dinner I went to bed. The radio was broadcasting a program on the "Lord's Prayer." I listened carefully. "Repeat after me," said the pastor, "Our Father...in heaven." And so it went on until he reached the phrase: "And forgive us our debts, *as we forgive our debtors.*" What happened next was the expected. Motivated by my earlier conversation with the young man, and concerned by his difficulty to forgive, God showed me a plank of unforgiveness that I had carried for eighteen years. When I repeated, "As we forgive our debtors," I saw in my mind, like in a movie, a scene between my mother and me. As a result of that incident I had been unable to forgive her.

When I was twelve years old, my father died. Thus my mom became a widow with eight children under her care. She never thought of getting married again, but when I was a teenager, there was a family friend like an "uncle," who would come to visit us and stay with my mom until late in the evenings. My brothers and sisters used to tease them, but I didn't find it funny at all. In my heart, my dad was irreplaceable. Even though I would say that my mom should remarry, I had not accepted the death of my father yet. One night we all went to bed, but I couldn't sleep. I was curious to know what my mom and my "uncle" were talking about downstairs in the kitchen. So I very quietly went downstairs. The door was closed, so I looked through the keyhole. I saw them kissing. It was like being stabbed. That image remained forever in my mind, along with bitterness, anger and unforgiveness. I never told anyone. It just stayed stuck in the depth of my being. In that moment, my life changed forever. I became rebellious. Although I was the best at school, I started to be the worst in the neighborhood. My life became drugs, alcohol and abandonment.

The pain of the young man at church and his ability to express it brought my unattended wound to the surface. "And forgive us our debts as we forgive our debtors," I repeated over and over again in my mind while seeing that old scene framed in the keyhole. I cried, and cried and cried some more. And in the meantime, a huge burden was removed from my shoulders. I forgave my mother for something she had never done, something that I would not forgive. The tears turned into joy and peace and love.

I have learned a lot lately. He who doesn't forgive destroys the bridge that God uses to come to us.

I have deliberately told you this story, so that you may understand how insistent the Holy Spirit is in revealing those areas in our life where we resist the Potter's hand. In this particular case, we find a sensitive heart ready to forgive. But some people will respond to the Potter's touch by hardening their hearts and ending up in destruction.

THE END OF YOUR FAILURE

The end of your failure is called the Holy Spirit. The Potter is ready to start working again to complete His perfect work in all those willing to surrender entirely to Him. We must allow the Lord to do unto us according to His will. Pray these words of surrender:

You are the Potter; I am the clay. I want to be soft and humble. May Your will be done in me. Try my heart, O Lord; wash me and remove all evil from me so that I can be truly Yours. Do unto me according to Your will; heal my wounds and my pain. Yours, O Lord, is the power; extend Your hand and heal me. Anoint me with Your Holy Spirit, O Master of my life, that the world may see Christ in me.

When you say these words, God may possibly say to you, "And what about that area in your life where you have been resisting My will?"

Respond to Him with these words:

It is Yours, Lord; I'll give it to You forever.

Then your life will be restored and changed in such a way that God's dream, His design, will be completed in you.

Naturally, the devil will try to hinder your consecration. He will tell you, "Don't be a fanatic. If you surrender, you will turn into a repressed and embittered person. You will lose everything you have." This is a lie. Imagine that you have a disobedient child who says, "From now on, I will obey you in everything. I will do whatever you ask me to do." Would you even think, *Now that I can have my way with him, I will afflict him and make him suffer, repressing him and forcing him to do all the things he hates to do, making sure that he is unhappy?* Of course not.

If my son came to me with words like that, I would say to my wife, "Betty, our son wants to obey us in everything! What are the good things that make him happy? I want to encourage him to do those. Is there anything that hurts him? He needs to leave that behind, but we will help him so that he doesn't get hurt unnecessarily."

My wife would also say, "Yes, Claudio, we will do everything we possibly can to make his life beautiful." Wouldn't you do the same? So if we then, though we are evil, know how to do good things for our children, how much more will our Father in heaven do for them?

The key is to be obedient. We have to be like the ashes that remain after a fire. Ashes go with the wind and follow its direction obediently. This is how we should be. The fire of God has to consume us spiritually until we are nothing but ashes, until there is nothing resisting His will. Then we can tell Him, "Lord, I am nothing but ashes. Breathe your Holy Spirit on me, and I will go wherever You want me to go."

The secret for a victorious Christian life is very simple. The Christian life is to allow God to carry us and lead us. It is allowing the Holy Spirit of God to manage, control and rule us. It is about experiencing a change. You don't direct yourself any longer; you allow the Lord to carry you in whatever way He wants, when He wants, where He wants and for whatever He wants.

Charles Finney, one of God's key men in the history of revivals, said, "A revival is nothing other than a new beginning with God...it is about a brokenness of heart, bowing before God in profound humility, and it is about leaving sin behind." This is true, not only at the collective level, or in the life of a church, city or nation. It is also true of our personal lives. In order for renewal and restoration to take place in our lives, we have to have a new start in our relationship with God. Let our hearts be broken, and let us bow down before His presence in complete humility, putting aside all pride and resistance and leaving the practice of sin behind.

In order for restoration to take place in your life, you have to give God absolute control. He wants to do a sovereign work in your life. He wants to accomplish His will in you so that His perfect design may be achieved in your life.

Arthur Wallis says that a revival is God's intervention in the normal course of the spiritual things. It is God revealing Himself to man in solemn holiness

and irresistible power. It is such a manifest intervention of God that human personalities get lost in the
shadow and human programs are abandoned. It is
man moving to the back, because God is on stage. It
is God bearing forth his arm and doing amazing
things for saints and sinners alike.

We all want a personal restoration, a church renewal and a massive conversion of unbelievers. We
all want revival. But are we willing to pay the price?
Are we willing to stop resisting and surrender to the
Potter's hands so that He can do His work in us?

When an army is being defeated, its commanding
officer has to make a crucial decision— resist or surrender. When we realize we are failing, God places
that same decision before us—resist or surrender.
The difference is that in God's wise designs, to surrender is equal to victory while resisting inevitably
leads us to defeat. Stop resisting and surrender to
the Lord. The Potter shows you His pierced hands
and says, "Let Me put My hands on you to shape you
again."

I want to lead you in a prayer that will change your
life. While you read it, repeat it aloud. Don't say the
words as if they were magic or without thinking what
they mean. That would be worthless. Repeat them as
if they were coming from within you. Say them with
all your heart. Pray with sincerity. Do not limit yourself to these few lines, but let the Holy Spirit pray for
you with groans that words cannot express. Let Him

guide your prayer and unveil your heart before the Lord's throne of grace.

Heavenly Father,

I love You. I come before You with repentance. I repent for each and every one of my sins. I repent for not having allowed You to rule my life. I repent for having resisted Your will. I repent for becoming hard in Your hands and for preventing Your wise hands to mold me according to Your will. I sincerely repent. Please forgive me, my beloved Lord. I hand the control of my life over to You, and I completely surrender to You. Divine Potter, mold me as You will. Do whatever You want with me, Lord.

Now let the Holy Spirit continue to guide your prayer. Don't run away from His presence. Stay there before Him. When you have no more words to say, just remain silent, expecting to hear Him speaking to you. He wants to do something in you now because you are back in the Potter's hands.

The vessels of the young men were holy, though it was an ordinary journey; how much more then today will their vessels be holy?

—1 SAMUEL 21:5, NAS

Ex. 34:10-17 / Joshua 9:

1 1

Holy Jars

IN THIS ILLUSTRATION from the twenty-first chapter of 1 Samuel, David arrives at Nob, escaping from Saul's persecution. Ahimelech the priest is there, and David asks him for food for himself and his men. The priest, surprised by his visit, tells him that the only bread available is the consecrated bread, which he was willing to give it to David's men if the men were purified. David tells him that his men, even though their journey was not a military campaign, had already been sanctified.

There was a provision in the Law that whoever was impure could not go to war. Deuteronomy 23:9 says, "When you are encamped against your enemies, keep away from everything impure." The victory in battle directly depended on the people's state of purification and sanctification.

Sanctification is a permanent and universal

imperative for God's people. It isn't a temporary and fashionable thing. Holiness has always been the church's biggest challenge, and how much more at the End Times! We are coming into the last revival in history. This is the time of our final confrontation against the forces of evil. God can't use us unless we are sanctified. If we are holy vessels, the enemy will not be able to prevail against us.

John Wesley, that great man of God used mightily by Him in major revivals, once said, "What hinders the work of God? I believe we do. If we would be holy, totally consecrated to God, wouldn't we preachers be on fire and spreading that fire across the nation?"

Before hearing God's voice calling him to attend to the needs of the people, the prophet Isaiah was confronted with his own sin. He saw the Lord in all His glory, and not taking it lightly, he broke down and confessed his sin. There is no bigger hindrance to the manifestation of God's power and to overcoming the forces of evil than sin.

We not only have to be holy to fight against the forces of evil, but we also have to fight the forces of evil in order to be holy. It is not a mere play on words. I would like to share with you a story that is found in Joshua 9:3–15. It will help you to understand the need to have your guard up when fighting for our holiness.

As we examine Israel's campaign, we can see how

carefully Joshua planned Canaan's conquest. He started by introducing a wedge from Jericho to the west, to the center of the land, with the purpose of dividing the enemies' opposition. Then he turned south to destroy the enemy in that direction, ending up later with the opposition in the north. It was an accurately planned military campaign.

The problem we have is that we read these passages as simple stories of Israel's history. Even though the secret to win a war lies in its strategy, we frequently do not apply the divine strategy to our daily lives. When we live our lives ignoring who our enemy is, or we don't recognize that we are in the midst of battle and need some strategy, we miss the target.

We have to be alert to Satan's schemes. He not only is our enemy, but also a master strategist. He is not just a roaring lion (1 Pet. 5:8), but also a shrewd serpent (2 Cor. 11:3). We may be ready to face a roaring lion, but not a serpent that in a very subtle way deceives us.

This passage in the Book of Joshua may help to illustrate how subtle the enemy can truly be and how easily we may be tricked. It also demonstrates how God's sovereignty turns everything for His glory in spite of our mistakes. After the Israelites' many victories, their enemies got ready for a major counterattack:

Now when all the kings west of the Jordan

heard about these things—those in the hill country, in the western foothills, and along the entire coast of the Great Sea as far as Lebanon (the kings of the Hittites, Amorites, Canaanites, Perizzites, Hivites and Jebusites)—they came together to make war against Joshua and Israel.

—JOSHUA 9:1–2

Every battle won by the believer in his personal life is an open invitation for the enemy's counterattack. Whenever a true child of God has a blessed experience, he can expect Satan to attack. Our blessings and battles go together. If you are surrounded by the enemy and find yourself in the center of the battle, praise the Lord! If the temptation is almost stronger than what you can endure, I'm glad. If you are burdened by temptations all around you, it is because you are advancing according to God's will.

On the other hand, if your experience is that Satan hasn't attacked you in years, then it is time for you to bow before the Lord so that He can tell you what is wrong with you. Your life may be so stuck that the devil isn't even interested in you.

As you read this chapter, you will understand better how Satan attacks us to prevent us from living in holiness.

THE ENEMY'S STRATEGY IS FOR US TO MAKE A TREATY WITH HIM

The people of Gibeon, instead of attacking Israel, chose to trick the Israelites into making a treaty with them. The Gibeonites arrived at Gilgal pretending to come from far away, from a place beyond Joshua's authority. They wore patched sandals, old and dirty clothes and carried cracked and mended wineskins. The most important element of their whole strategy was to declare that they deeply respected, honored and believed in the God of the Israelites.

This is typical of Satan's methodology. He knows very well that a consecrated believer will not give in to a frontal attack. He knows that a child of God who walks with the Lord and who is standing on blessed ground will always be alert and will not fall into an open attack. So what does Satan do? He talks about possible treaties: "Make a treaty with us" (Josh. 9:6).

Obviously, in every treaty, each side will accept and give into conditions imposed by the other. In this case, they are nothing important; they seem like nothing in comparison to our devotion to the Lord. He challenges us in regards to our total consecration to God by saying, "Come on, don't take it so seriously. Don't be so narrow-minded and so enthusiastic about it. Don't be a fanatic." He actually insinuates that certain areas of our life are not under Jesus' authority.

It is important to know that the devil will always

say that he believes in God. The Bible says that "even the demons believe...and shudder" (James 2:19).

What are his conditions in the treaty? He suggests that we should be more practical in money issues, and that in our financial dealings we have to be pragmatic rather than obedient to God. Regarding love, he says that what matters is our feelings and the people we like. It really doesn't matter if he or she is a believer. The important thing is that you like that person and feel something for him or her.

Do you realize what I'm saying? If you truly are a Christian, the devil will not attack you head-on, but will try to make treaties with you. If you have a business, he will try to remove it from under God's absolute control. He will also try to prevent young people who are entering into a relationship from making Jesus Christ Lord of their emotional life. He will whisper in their ear, "Go ahead, don't worry; he or she will eventually become a Christian." And he will even affirm his suggestions with Bible verses such as, "You and your house will be saved." When attacking, he always uses half-truths. Undoubtedly, there are possibilities for that person to become a Christian, but it isn't necessarily going to be that way. The promise, as with all biblical promises, is conditioned upon our obedience to God's will.

It's the same in church. He tells us to be practical and not to take the Bible so seriously, but to have some common sense. And yet the Bible declares,

"Do not believe every spirit, but test the spirits to see whether they are from God" (1 John 4:1).

We need to be alert to Satan's schemes. He wants to make treaties with us to prevent us from being completely holy.

THE ENEMY'S STRATEGY IS BASED ON OUR FOOLISHNESS

The devil tempts us, but we are the ones responsible for our fall. We can't shield ourselves saying, "Oh well, it was Satan who tempted me; he is so clever..." We are responsible. The following verse is very important: "The men of Israel sampled their provisions but *did not inquire of the LORD*" (Josh. 9:14, emphasis added).

We never seem to understand how vital it is to read our Bibles and pray. When we don't, we encounter difficulties, and the spirit of discernment is destroyed. The voice of the hireling sounds a lot like the voice of the Shepherd. Satan disguises himself as an angel of light to confuse, deceive and draw us apart from the authentic consecration of holiness unto the Lord.

Unfortunately, many believers have realized too late that those things that seemed unimportant have ruined their lives. As the Bible says, "Catch for us the foxes, the little foxes that ruin the vineyards, our vineyards that are in bloom" (Song of Sol. 2:15). It is not the big things in our life that ruin our relationship with God, but the little foxes. They are the ones that ruin the vineyards. Those unimportant things are the ones that contaminate and prevent us from living in holiness.

Those things that seem insignificant to us are a little open door to Satan. When it remains open, he enters with his persuasive words, and we fall. Many live in failure because of not inquiring of the Lord! So many believers end in bankruptcy after making business treaties with unbelievers! So many make a treaty with an unbeliever and get married. Then they spend the rest of their lives suffering for not having been able to live out the Christian ideal or because they can't share with their spouse the thing they love the most. They cry and groan for their spouse's conversion, after living forty years with someone who didn't help them worship and serve the Lord!

We begin to inquire of the Lord by turning to His Word. The Bible is not there just to be admired, memorized or praised for its wisdom. The Bible is the voice of God, and we have to obey it. When we don't find in it the answer we need for our particular situation, we inquire of God through prayer. Reading the Bible and praying always go together in order to hear God's voice. Christians who don't read the Bible and pray are listening to the devil's voice or to the voice of their own hearts.

When believers around the world ask me, "Pastor Claudio, what do I have to do when facing a decision in my life?" my usual answer is, "Don't trust in your own understanding." Your common sense may seem to indicate that a certain path is good, and it could be so. But it could also happen that the path of blessing is completely opposite to our common sense.

In 1985, God spoke to me through a vision, telling me to leave my ministry in Parque Chás to start a new church in the aristocratic neighborhood of Belgrano in the city of Buenos Aires. At that moment, His will for my life seemed to make no sense at all. After so many years of sowing in dry ground, our little church was finally full of people and anointed by the Holy Spirit. And now God was asking us to move? It didn't make any sense. Not even my loved ones could understand it. But God had clearly spoken to me.

One morning, He suddenly woke me up and showed me a vision on the wall. I saw a park in Belgrano called Plaza Noruega. In the vision, the park was full of people holding an evangelistic crusade. The Lord told me, "This is your new work camp." It was a very difficult and challenging situation for me. No one else had received this vision. But I decided to be faithful to my convictions.

I planned a crusade for that park. That crusade was very successful; hundreds of people got saved, and signs and wonders accompanied their testimonies. I had never experienced anything like it.

That is how the King of Kings Church in Belgrano was born. Today it has more than six thousand members. It also has a powerful revival and evangelization ministry that has spread to the rest of the world. Truly, God's will is pleasing and perfect! But it has to be found, not through our minds or human understanding, but on our knees.

It is very important to discern God's voice. When we hear voices telling us to act immediately, first inquire of the Lord. If there are still doubts, let us be still. If we are told to act but we haven't prayed, let us not do it. We are not supposed to do anything until God's peace confirms what we should do.

Be strong and courageous enough to be still and wait on God, because those who wait on the Lord will never be put to shame (Ps. 25:3).

THE ENEMY'S STRATEGY IS TO CONVINCE US THAT WE ARE DEFEATED PERMANENTLY

While reading this chapter, you may have realized that you have made a mistake, that you have actually made treaties in your business and in your marriage, and you're suffering because of it. At the same time you may be thinking that it is too late now, that there is no solution. I want to tell you that it is all a lie of the enemy. It is part of his strategy to get the believer to make mistakes, so that he can whisper in his ear, "It's too late; you are defeated."

See what verse 21 of Joshua 9 says: "They [the leaders] continued, 'Let them live, but let them be woodcutters and water carriers for the entire community.' So the leaders' promise to them was kept." I think this is wonderful. We can lose battles. Who doesn't? We can be wrong. Our jar may be cracked. But the last word belongs to the Lord. Hallelujah!

The Gibeonites had to cut wood for the fire on the altar and carry water to be used in the temple rituals for the people of Israel. The deceivers were humiliated in such a way that they had to light the fire at the altar and be the means of purification for the worship of God.

If possible, break right now any treaty done in disobedience to God.

Obviously, if a believer has made a marital treaty with a Gibeonite, he won't be able to break it. In that case, what should he do? The Bible says, "If any brother has a wife who is not a believer and she is willing to live with him, he must not divorce her. And if a woman has a husband who is not a believer and he is willing to live with her, she must not divorce him. . . . How do you know, wife, whether you will save your husband? Or, how do you know, husband, whether you will save your wife?" (1 Cor. 7:12–16).

That means that we are not supposed to abandon our commitment. But the Bible also teaches that if we come in humility, acknowledging that we have disobeyed, that we have sinned, the Lord will make the Gibeonite the means by which we come closer to God in prayer. When confessed with all sincerity,

God will use that sin in our lives as a means to strengthen our prayer life and deepen our devotion. If this is your situation, you can pray like this:

Lord,

I'm sorry for my mistakes and for my disobedience. I believe You can restore the years that the locusts have eaten. I will not allow Satan to drag me down and enslave me. I want "Gibeonite" to be the means to bring me closer to You in prayer. Forgetting what lies behind, I will try hard to do Your will in the future.

May God help you realize, as many other believers have, that the very things you have done wrong may be the things that bring you daily to the feet of the cross of Jesus Christ. God can transform the sin that held us prisoners into the means to come closer to Him.

Our struggle to be holy is not against flesh and blood, but against Satan. Let us recognize our enemy; let us know we are in the midst of a battle and consider his strategies. Let us overcome him in the power of the Holy Spirit with a life completely consecrated to Him. Let us be holy vessels in the hands of the Potter. Then we will not only be holy, but we will go to war ready to overcome our enemy so the world may come to know our Lord.

What if God, although willing to demonstrate His wrath and to make His power known, endured with much patience vessels of wrath prepared for destruction?

—ROMANS 9:22, NAS

1 2

Restored Jars

RESTORATION IS NOT something that takes place in an instant. The Potter will submit our lives to a long process of shaping us.

When we accept our need for restoration and place ourselves in His hands, God takes our intention very seriously and starts to shape us. If we are entirely surrendered, our whole existence will be restored—not just one aspect of it.

Because I want you to be able to understand this process, I will tell you about a particular situation that appears in the Bible in 2 Chronicles, chapter 33. It is the story of Manasseh. I chose the story of this king of Judah as an example because his was one of the worst lives we could ever find. It is the story of someone who fell really low because of his sin. I would like you to see that no matter how low we fall, if we are willing to place ourselves in the hands of the Potter, He takes us just as we are and restores us. If He did it with Manasseh, how much more will He do it with us?

Manasseh started to reign when he was only twelve years old, and he ruled for fifty-five years. The chronicler divides his reign into two parts. In the first one, Manasseh was filled with only sin and evil deeds. The biblical writer bluntly summarizes this period by saying, "He did evil in the eyes of the LORD, following the detestable practices of the nations the LORD had driven out before the Israelites" (v. 2). His behavior was in stark contrast to that of his father, Hezekiah. After David, Hezekiah was the godliest of all the kings of Judah. Manasseh, his son, came to be the most heathen of them all.

MANASSEH'S FALL

The description of his reign is very harsh. The Word of God says that he followed the same practices of the Canaanites. His reign was the utmost expression of paganism: "He rebuilt the high places his father Hezekiah had demolished; he also erected altars to the Baals and made Asherah poles. He bowed down to all the starry hosts and worshiped them" (v. 3). His father Hezekiah had removed the high places (2 Kings 18:4).

But Manasseh rebuilt them and even erected altars to the Baals and Asherah. He worshiped all

164

the starry hosts, introducing to Judah the whole Assyrian pantheon—the starry hosts, the sun, the moon, the goddess Ishtar and all other members of that astral religion.

As if this weren't enough, Manasseh "sacrificed his sons in the fire in the Valley of Ben Hinnom, practiced sorcery, divination and witchcraft, and consulted mediums and spiritists" (2 Chron. 33:6). He not only erected altars in God's temple, but sacrificed his own sons in the fire. He made them go through the fire, according to a typical Caananite pagan ritual. The Canaanites would kill their sons and burn them as a burnt offering to the god Molech.

He practiced the reading of clouds and the interpretation of their different shapes in order to predict the future. God naturally forbade this practice. It was the equivalent to practicing astrology and divination, both condemned practices in Deuteronomy 18:9–14 and Leviticus 19:26–31. He practiced necromancy, or the conjuration of the spirits of the dead, severely forbidden by God in Deuteronomy 18:11. He also practiced different kinds of magic.

God's report on Manasseh was that he went beyond the limits of evil: "He did much evil in the eyes of the LORD, provoking him to anger" (2 Chron. 33:6). He placed the carved image he had made *in God's temple.* It was a statue of Asherah and her entourage that represented masculine and feminine religious prostitution. (See 2 Kings 23:7.)

He not only carried his evil deeds to an extreme, but also "led Judah and the people of Jerusalem astray, so that they did more evil than the nations the LORD had destroyed before the Israelites" (2 Chron. 33:9). Such degree of paganism and demonization caused the priests and prophets to react, and they announced the punishment that would reach Jerusalem. But instead of listening to the prophetic exhortation, Manasseh drowned those voices in blood (2 Kings 21:16). Tradition tells us that among his innocent victims was Isaiah, who may have died sawed in two by the king's orders (Heb. 11:37).

Because of Manasseh's wickedness and disobedience, God brought judgment against him and his people: "So the LORD brought against them the army commanders of the king of Assyria, who took Manasseh prisoner, put a hook in his nose, bound him with bronze shackles and took him to Babylon" (2 Chron. 33:11).

He was surely an evil king, the most godless of the whole history of Judah, controlled by the forces of evil, capable of committing all kinds of idolatry, occultism, Satanism, murders, including the ritual death of his own children. He also led his own people astray. Could this evil man, capable of igniting God's wrath, be restored? Could this king, shackled and tied by the Assyrians and by Satan himself, be freed and restored?

MANASSEH'S RESTORATION

Manasseh ended up as a captive in Babylon, shackled with a hook in his nose. And yet, we are surprised by the miracle of divine restoration, God's incomprehensible compassion and love. At the worst time in a man's life, when he is deep in the mire, God extends His hand and gives him a second chance. The Potter takes the clay and places it back on the wheel to restore it.

There are certain steps to consider in this whole process of restoration.

Restoration of hearing God's voice

The restoration of hearing God's voice is the first step in this process of reconstruction. Verse 10 speaks not only about God's patience and mercy in always giving second chances, but it also explains what caused Manasseh and his people to fall: "The LORD spoke to Manasseh and his people, but they paid no attention." So the first thing to be restored is our ability to hear God's voice. Manasseh knew about God, but he didn't want to listen to what He had to say. His father, Hezekiah, had taught him the ways of the Lord, and yet Manasseh refused to listen to God. He eventually moved away from his father's instruction and started to walk his own path.

It is very important to determine the moment we have moved away from God's direction, the moment when we stopped listening to His voice in order to follow our own.

In 2 Kings, chapter 6, there is an interesting story in the ministry of the prophet Elisha. The company of the prophets went with Elisha to cut wood to build a place to live, because the place where they were was too small for them. As one of them was cutting down a tree, the iron ax he was using fell into the river Jordan. Desperate, this man moaned the loss, since the ax that had fallen into the water was borrowed. Elisha cut a stick and threw it into the water. Miraculously, the iron floated and the ax was recovered. But, before the miracle, Elisha asked these men the following key question: "Where did it fall?"

He didn't throw the stick just anywhere in the river. It was fundamental to know exactly where the ax had fallen in order for the miracle of recovery to take place.

I ask you the same question today: "Where did you fall?" In other words, what moved you away from God? When did you stop listening to and obeying His voice? In order for God to perform a miracle of restoration in your life, you have to go back to that place, that moment in your life when you pulled away. It doesn't matter that the waters in the river have continued to flow. It doesn't matter that it happened a long time ago. It doesn't matter that the ax's heavy weight has sent it to the bottom of the river. You shouldn't even think: *I can't go back; I have sunk too deep.* God performed the miracle to recover the ax, and God will perform a miracle of restoration in your life. Go back to the place where you fell and start to hear His voice once again.

Restoration of prayer

The second step in this process is the restoration of prayer. Manasseh finally set his self-sufficiency aside and prayed to God: "In his distress he sought the favor of the LORD his God and humbled himself greatly before the God of his fathers" (2 Chron. 33:12). Obviously, Manasseh had to be put back on the Potter's wheel to go through pain and tribulation. Due to his hard and resistant heart, he had to suffer much in captivity. He needed to turn from his pride to God. So finally he humbled himself before the Lord.

But there are many individuals who will not leave their self-sufficiency behind and turn to the Lord, not even in the midst of anguish. They know they need God, and that He is the only way out, but they keep trying to take care of themselves, saying, "I'm not going to turn to God now just because I'm anguished and in captivity. First I need to get my act together again, and then I will return to Him—out of love and not out of interest." Underneath it all they are saying that they want to save themselves, without God's intervention. Then they'll go to the Lord, but by their own merits. What foolishness and pride!

While a captive, Manasseh, shackled and anguished, put his pride aside, turned to God and prayed. Now, realize that the one who prayed was the most godless king in the history of Judah. He committed the most sins. He got most involved in witchcraft and satanic cults. He killed his own sons in satanic rituals. And he not only sinned but also led his people astray. This king had provoked God's wrath like none other in his time.

Yet, watch what the result of his prayer was: "And when he prayed to him, the LORD was moved by his entreaty and listened to his plea; so he brought him back to Jerusalem and to his kingdom. Then Manasseh knew that the Lord is God" (v. 13). No matter what your situation before the Lord may be, if you truly humble yourself before His presence, His grace and His mercy will restore your life. It was necessary for Manasseh to humble himself.

It is not enough to recognize our bad condition and ask God to free us, bless us and heal us. In conjunction with the acknowledgment and petition, there has to be the desire to change. After all this, God will start looking into our future and not at our past. Instead of looking at our sins, He will pay attention to His plans for us. He will not look at the cracks on our jar, but rather concentrate on the wonderful piece of pottery that we were meant to be, even before the foundations of the world.

Manasseh was restored to Jerusalem and to his

kingdom. Therefore, not only was he freed from the Babylonian captivity, but he was also king again. This is what God does in our lives. He not only frees us from sin, but also restores us to our position of kings. When we return like the prodigal son to God our Father, He puts the best robe on us and a ring of authority on our finger (Luke 15:22).

Restoration of the wall

Manasseh's process of rehabilitation didn't end with his restoration, since Manasseh had to restore several things himself. It is very important for you to understand this, because many Christians who have been restored stop at that. As a result they end up worse than before. God restored them, but they didn't restore themselves. When God's work of restoration finishes, yours starts.

The restoration of the wall is something that you have to do. It is something that Manasseh did. God restored him, but Manesseh restored the wall: "Afterward he rebuilt the outer wall of the City of David, west of the Gihon spring in the valley, as far as the entrance of the Fish Gate and encircling the hill of Ophel; he also made it much higher. He stationed military commanders in all the fortified cities in Judah" (2 Chron. 33:14).

Once God has restored our lives, we have to raise a spiritual wall to protect ourselves from the enemy's attacks. The wall has to be solid, without any holes, so that the enemy will not be able to come in. Paul wrote a letter to the Ephesians, saying, "And do not give the devil a foothold" (Eph. 4:27). When we leave holes in the wall, when we don't put on the whole armor of God, Satan will find us defenseless and attack us again. Then he will achieve his goal—our condition will be worse than before.

Manasseh, having already abandoned all self-sufficiency and knowing that the enemy would try to attack him again, made a *much higher wall*. If you fill your daily life with the presence of the Holy Spirit, your wall will be very high also. The devil can't harm a believer who is full of the Holy Spirit.

Restoration of the altar

After he restored the wall, Manasseh next restored the altar. "Then he restored the altar of the LORD and sacrificed fellowship offerings and thank offerings on it" (2 Chron. 33:16). God will not restore your altar—you have to do it. Don't expect God to give you the desire to pray, read the Bible, worship and go to church. Christians don't do things because we feel like it; it is a matter of our will and obedience to God.

Leviticus 6:12 teaches us the following: "The fire on the altar must be kept burning; it must not go out. Every morning the priest is to add firewood and arrange the burnt offering on the fire and burn the fat of the fellowship offerings on it." The priest had to keep the fire burning, and it required a daily and constant effort. He had to get up early in the morning and sometimes walk a long distance to gather the wood. Then he had to add the wood, prepare the burnt offering and diligently watch the fire to make sure it did not go out. It was a hard task and demanded much responsibility. It wasn't a matter of feelings, but rather of effort and discipline, surrender and will. If we don't repair the altar, our restored life will be weak again.

Restoration of our giving

Once the altar was repaired, Manasseh restored his giving. He presented sacrifices and offerings. Many believers don't realize the importance of giving. They believe that their offering is to pay for the church or the ministry's expenses. In reality, the offering is a believer's worship and praise to God.

Restoration of our praise

In addition to sacrificing fellowship offerings, Manasseh also sacrificed thank offerings of praise, thus restoring praise. Praise is key in this process. Its purpose is not only to recognize God, thanking and glorifying Him, but it also operates in our heart. Praise alters the way we approach life. Many believers live in defeat because they listen to the news instead of praising God in the morning. Their minds are filled with negative, pessimistic and bitter thoughts. Praise fills us with joy when we understand

God's love for us. It fills us with hope, knowing that God will do His work in our circumstances and in us. It fills us with feelings of security, knowing that God loves us and is with us. Hallelujah! Restore your praise to God, and it will keep you healthy.

Restoration of our service

The last step in Manasseh's rehabilitation process is the restoration of service. "...and told Judah to serve the LORD the God of Israel" (2 Chron. 33:16). Our spare time is a hole the enemy will use to restart his work in us. When God restores us, we need to restore our service to Him. It is not a matter of feeling like it—it is a command. In the New American Standard Version of the Bible it says that Manasseh "ordered" Judah to serve the Lord.

Many Christians have a purely defensive attitude about the enemy and are worried only about his attacks. They restore the wall, but they don't restore the service. Instead of you being worried about the enemy, God wants the devil to be worried about you. He should be bothered by the way you witness, by those who are healed through your prayers, by your authority in rebuking his hosts and by your service in the church, building up Christ's body.

No vessel was worse than Manasseh. None was so proud, so disobedient, so evil and so dark. It ended up broken. But Manasseh had the wisdom to return to the Potter's hands. And in spite of all the cracks and chinks, the good Potter restored him to his place, his people and his authority as king. The Potter wants to do the same with you today. Follow Manasseh's steps, and your life will forever change.

Go down to the potter's house, and there I will give you my message.

—JEREMIAH 18:2

13

Outpoured Jars

THE LORD EXTENDS a solemn invitation to us. He invites us to go to the Potter's house. He wants to do a new thing there. But first of all we have to hear His message: "I will give you My message."

In 1992 my ministry life was intense. Every morning I would conduct an evangelistic radio program. Then later in the day I would work at the church office and do some pastoral counseling. At night, I would teach or preach at the meetings. I was working as much as fourteen hours a day, seven days a week. I was really busy with all the demands of an ever-growing church. And yet I felt something was missing. I had a need that was hard to identify.

One night, Pastor Werner Kniesel visited me. He is the pastor of the largest church in Switzerland and had been a missionary in Argentina. After many years, we met again, and he joined us in one of our church services. Then we went for dinner to eat that wonderful Argentinean meat that Werner missed so much in Europe. I started to tell him what God was doing in our lives. I told him about all my many activities. I honestly expected him to congratulate me. I thought that, after hearing about all that I was doing, he was going to say, "Oh, Claudio, how awesome to hear about all that God has given you and is doing in you!" However, he limited his comment to one question. It was a question that shook my life. He said, "Claudio, how much time do you devote to the Holy Spirit?"

When I heard that, I almost choked! Werner continued, "You have grown a lot, and the church is beautiful, but there is something wrong. The Holy Spirit wants to talk to you, and you have no time to listen."

From that moment on, I understood that before God can do anything with us, but we have to hear His voice. The Potter invites us to his house and says, "I shall announce My words to you" (NAS). What does He want to talk about? What are the things we need to hear before He can start His work in us and shape us according to His design? I believe that He first wants us to understand that this is the right time to experience a radical change. These are very special times, His Holy Spirit times.

When Simeon, a righteous and devout man upon

whom the Holy Spirit rested, took the child Jesus in his arms, he prayed and said: "Sovereign Lord, as you have promised, you now dismiss your servant in peace. For my eyes have seen your salvation, which you have prepared in the sight of all people" (Luke 2:29–31).

We didn't have the privilege to know Jesus in person, as Simeon did, and to hold Him in our arms. But we have a privilege that this man never had. He could catch a glimpse of the salvation that God was going to prepare in the sight of all people. But we will be able to see its fulfillment all over the earth. Hallelujah!

The prophet declared, "For the earth will be filled with the knowledge of the glory of the LORD, as the waters cover the sea" (Hab. 2:14). I believe that the time of the fulfillment of this prophecy is here. Simeon witnessed the beginning of that time, but we can participate in its fulfillment. How will the earth be filled with the knowledge of the glory of God? *Through us.*

YOU WILL REAP WHAT YOU SOWED

The psalmist says, "Those who sow in tears will reap with songs of joy. He who goes out weeping, carrying seed to sow, will return with songs of joy, carrying sheaves with him" (Ps. 126:5–6). You and I are the fruits of many who have sown in tears. But, we will reap what others have sown in tears. I lift a prayer of thanksgiving to the Lord for all those who came before us!

The psalmist is not talking, though, about two different kinds of people. He doesn't talk about the ones who sow and the ones who reap. The biblical author mentions just one group. Those who sow in tears are the ones who will reap with songs of joy. Those who carry the precious seed in tears will return with songs of joy, carrying sheaves in their arms.

I think that we need to ask ourselves: *Why does sowing the Word make us cry? Why is it so painful to share our faith with others?* If the Bible says that there is joy in the sharing of the Word, that the feet of those who proclaim that God reigns are beautiful, then why so much pain, why tears? Why is it so difficult to testify about our Lord?

I think that the Bible is realistic. Carrying God's Word can be costly. There can be the cost of having other people think that we are weird or something. There is the cost of overcoming our selfish thinking that the other person is not living the abundant life. The cost of backing our words with our actions. The spiritual cost of overcoming the barriers that Satan places before us to keep us from speaking to or interceding for the lost. Ultimately, there is the cost of denying ourselves.

Fearing other people's rejection, feeling shame and selfishness, are all subtle forms of pride. Saying we do not have the ability to do what we have to do may also be a form of pride. It is the Holy Spirit—and not us—who does the work.

Sharing the Word may be painful; it even can make us cry, because we have to deny ourselves. There is definitely a price to pay. Even those who have the gift of evangelism will tell you that there is a price to pay. It not only requires us to deny ourselves, but also to overcome the evil one. There are times when you can't share the gospel, not because of your inability, but because the devil, knowing that God is using you to bless others, will try to stop you from doing your job. We have to discern who our enemy is and then put on the whole armor of God, stand firm and announce the gospel of peace.

This time of reaping is a time of joy. In the past many could only sow. But we are the people to whom the psalm refers. We are in a time of sowing and reaping. This is harvest time, so our mouths are filled with laughter, and our tongues are unceasingly praising our God.

In these days the lost will recognize what God has done in your life. As soon as you share your testimony, people will say, "The LORD has done great things for them" (Ps. 126:2). Like Simeon, thank God for allowing you to live in a time like this. (See Luke 2:28–32.) These are the times that Joel prophesied about when he said that God would send the latter rain and a great harvest (Joel 2:23). It is the time

Zechariah announced when he said, "Ask the LORD for rain in the springtime; it is the LORD who makes the storm clouds. He gives showers of rain to men, and plants of the field to everyone" (Zech. 10:1).

This is a time to rejoice and be glad. Isaiah says to you, "Sing, O barren woman, you who never bore a child; burst into song, shout for joy" (Isa. 54:1). Joel tells you, "Be glad, O people of Zion, rejoice in the LORD your God, for he has given you the autumn rains in righteousness. He sends you abundant showers, both autumn and spring rains, as before" (Joel 2:23). Habakkuk says, "Yet I will rejoice in the LORD I will be joyful in God my Savior" (Hab. 3:18). And Zechariah says to you, "Rejoice greatly, O Daughter of Zion! Shout, Daughter of Jerusalem!... The fasts of the fourth, fifth, seventh and tenth months will become joyful and glad occasions and happy festivals for Judah" (Zech. 9:9; 8:19). Therefore rejoice, be glad, celebrate and praise because God has chosen you to fill the earth with the knowledge of His glory. This is your time! It is the time of the Holy Spirit on the earth, and He wants to anoint you to go forth and fill the earth with the knowledge of Him.

Jesus Christ said, "Go into all the world and preach the good news to all creation" (Mark 16:15). Do you think you can do it? It is not for "specialists"; it is for you. When someone is sick, will you pray for his healing? Praying for the sick is not a task that only a "few" can do; it is something you can do, too. Will you set Satan's prisoners free? Don't say in your heart, "I can't do it." Rather say, "I can do all things in Christ." Then go and do it. Jesus promised this:

> And these signs will accompany those who believe: In my name they will drive out demons; they will speak in new tongues; they will pick up snakes with their hands; and when they drink deadly poison, it will not hurt them at all; they will place their hands on sick people, and they will get well.
>
> —MARK 16:17–18

People will be saved, healed, delivered and blessed by your participation in the move of God at this time. You have everything you need; the Holy Spirit is over you and inside of you and wants to work through you for the glory of the Lord.

A TEN-DAY WAIT

The Book of Acts tells us that there were ten days between Jesus' ascension and the coming of the Holy Spirit over the disciples. Why so many days? Probably the disciples were feeling like soldiers forced to stop in the middle of a battle because their general is gone. They were terribly confused and not sure of what to do.

They went back to the upper room where they had met so often with Jesus. Maybe some of them were hoping that He would show up once more, just as He had in those forty days after His death and resurrection. But the days went by, and He didn't come. The promise of the coming of the Holy Spirit wasn't being fulfilled, either. Maybe some even wondered, *If we couldn't win while He was with us, what chances do we have without Him?*

But the question was, why ten days? Because they had to wait until the Feast of Pentecost. God had decided that Jesus had to die on the Feast of Passover, since He symbolized the Lamb that takes away the sins of the world. The Passover lamb is also a reminder of the liberation of God's people from slavery in Egypt. Likewise, they had to wait for the Feast of Pentecost for the Holy Spirit to descend, because that feast symbolized the harvest's firstfruits. And so it happened: The day of the Harvester—the Holy Spirit—arrived, and three thousand souls were gathered as firstfruits of the kingdom of God.

Pentecost is the beginning of the End Times. They begin with the coming of the Holy Spirit and continue until the Second Coming of Jesus. We are in the midst of those last days. This is the Holy Spirit's time; it is harvest time. The Harvester has come to convict the world of sin and judgment. Peter explained what had happened by saying that the outpouring of the Holy Spirit was the fulfillment of the prophecy of Joel.

Truly during Pentecost the fulfillment of that prophecy started. Obviously the prophecy wasn't completely accomplished. God is preparing history's greatest revival. It is the revival that will precede the rapture of the church.

God is preparing His church for the coming revival by the renewal of the Holy Spirit. We can't go through Pentecost again, just as we couldn't go through Calvary again. But we can grab hold of the power that was present during Pentecost with the same assurance that we can grab hold of the redemption that Calvary provided for us.

Unfortunately many Christians don't know the difference between having the Holy Spirit and being filled by Him. From the moment of our conversion, the Holy Spirit abides in us. But we have to be constantly filled by Him. That is why the fullness of the Spirit is something we need to seek daily.

God is filling us with His Holy Spirit. He is anointing His church for the coming revival. Would you like to be a part of the revival generation that precedes the coming of the Lord? If you want revival, you have to know that revival starts with you.

When Moody went to England, a good friend told him, "Moody, the world is ready to see what God can do through a man who surrenders to Him." In Moody's biography, this friend shares that Moody, with great humility, answered him, "I will be that man."

Moody had no formal education. His English wasn't polished and perfect. He was never ordained as a minister, but he was a man that made the United States and Europe tremble because he was full of the Holy Spirit and ready to surrender to the Lord's hands.

We are at the End Times. God wants to use you, no matter what your circumstances are or the condition you are in. That is the reason He needs to fill you with His Holy Spirit. You may have had a spiritual experience ten years ago—or five, or last Sunday. But that is over. Yesterday's anointing is not good for today. God wants to fill your life today, giving you a fresh, new and powerful anointing.

Revival starts with you. It is personal first, then it goes to the church and finally it affects the whole world. We can't go into the world before going to God first. Some want to do the work of God without knowing the God of the work. Some want to be jars used by God without going through His workshop. Impossible. Today you have to go to the Potter's house and tell God, "Lord, I want to be filled with the Holy Spirit because I need a fresh anointing in order to serve You and bless those around me."

This anointing that God is pouring on us is not for us to keep, but to be used in this last revival. Some years ago when God anointed me in an incredible way, I thought that the experience was just for my church and me. But the Holy Spirit immediately told me, "Claudio, I want you to share this fresh anointing with all the pastors and all the churches." Since then, thousands upon thousands have received the fresh touch of God through our ministry. God never wants His works to remain in our lives. Whatever He gives is for us first, but then, right away, we have to share it with others so that the world may know of His love.

Various reports from all over the world confirm what the president of a Latin American organization wrote to me one day: "There is spiritual revival in many congregations all over our country. Many pastors have experienced a renewal in their ministries, and incredible things are happening. Many of the pastors' wives have testified that they have a new husband. They have experienced unbelievable changes in their lives and ministries. Our churches are not big enough to hold the people God is touching and who come searching for Him. We firmly believe that the Holy Spirit has found a place in many ministers who are thirsty for His presence." Do you realize what God can do when we place ourselves in His hands? Do you realize that God wants to do something in you so that you can be a blessing to others?

God fills you with His Holy Spirit because He needs you. He is raising new men and women to be part of the revival He is bringing forth to us. Today He is calling you. We are living a new stage in the life of the church of Jesus Christ. It is the time to seek

God and to respond to His calling. It is the time when men and women are called to fulfill their mission and to be part of the coming revival. Our sons and daughters will prophesy, our young people will see visions and our old men will dream dreams.

This is God's time. His time has arrived. Don't let your own clock be slow, but rather be in sync with God's. This is God's time, the time of the latter rains, the time of the harvest. Neither you nor your children should be excluded from this move. God is calling you to be one of the last-hour workers. God calls you to act jointly with Him, participating in His work.

That is why the Potter wants to work in your life. That is why He invites you to His house. You have already heard His words: "This is My time and your time." Now, He is expecting you to say, "Mold me, Lord, and use me."

And Moses sent them, a thousand from each tribe, to the war, and Phinehas the son of Eleazar the priest, to the war with them, and the holy vessels and the trumpets for the alarm in his hand.
—NUMBERS 31:6, NAS

14

Jars of War

IN NUMBERS 31 we read of Moses' last feat of war
before his death. It is the fulfillment of an order
received from God, who commanded Moses to
destroy the Midianites due to their hostility toward
Israel and the ongoing seduction in matters of worship. Through the Midianite's women, Israel was
drawn into sin, thus provoking the wrath of God
(Num. 25:18).

God's wrath is not just a symbol or a simple figure
of speech. It is a terrible fact that becomes a reality
in the face of evil. God wants to punish Midian for
their seduction and arrogance. Midian is a represen-
tation of Satan and his evil hosts, always trying to
induce others to sin. In their arrogance, they try to
deceive and humiliate God's people. The word
Midian means "struggle" and symbolizes our permanent struggle with Satan.

It is interesting to denote that Phinehas, son of Eleazar the priest, carries with him two elements. One of them is trumpets. That makes sense, since they needed them to indicate when to start the battle and move forward towards the enemy. But the second element has little to do with war. The Word says that he carried the vessels of the sanctuary.

VESSELS OF WAR

When Jesus called His disciples, He had two purposes in mind: "He appointed twelve— designating them apostles—that they might be with him and that he might send them out to preach and to have authority to drive out demons" (Mark 3:14–15). That is, Jesus called them to have intimate communion with Him, but He also sent them to the battlefield to preach with authority and to defeat the devil.

This double purpose is still valid for us today. The Potter keeps on shaping us to make us into vessels of the sanctuary, jars that serve Him in worship and close communion. But He also wants to send us to war. He takes your life, a sanctuary vessel, and wants to take you to the battlefield in order to win the victory.

God's people are a people at war. Paul urged the Philippians to stand firm in one spirit, contending as one man for the faith of the gospel: "Whatever happens, conduct yourselves in a manner worthy of the gospel of Christ. Then, whether I come and see you or only hear about you in my absence, I will know that you stand firm in one spirit, contending as one man for the faith of the gospel" (Phil. 1:27). He challenged the Ephesians: "Put on the full armor of God so that you can take your stand against the devil's schemes. For our struggle is not against flesh and blood, but against the rulers, against the authorities, against the powers of this dark world and against the spiritual forces of evil in the heavenly realms" (Eph. 6:11–12).

He reminds the Corinthians what their resources were: "For though we live in the world, we do not wage war as the world does. The weapons we fight with are not the weapons of the world. On the contrary, they have divine power to demolish strongholds. We demolish arguments and every pretension that sets itself up against the knowledge of God, and we take captive every thought to make it obedient to Christ" (2 Cor. 10:3–5). Like it or not, we are in the midst of battle. But God has given us the weapons to win, not only in our lives, but also in the lives of others.

EXERCISE YOUR SPIRITUAL AUTHORITY

The Old Testament is full of stories of wars and battles. These stories have been inspired by the Holy Spirit not just to inform us about Israel's history, but also to teach us about our own wars. Among these episodes, the capture of Jericho is probably one of the best known and also one of the most instructive.

The unusual strategy God gave the children of Israel had an intelligent purpose. To march in silence around a wall for several days didn't have a clear military sense. What was its purpose? Its purpose was that the people would obtain spiritual authority by exercising their faith, obedience and self-control.

We also have to affirm our spiritual authority. We don't live in an amusement park—we are in the midst of war. We don't fight against other human beings, but against rulers, authorities, powers of this dark world and spiritual forces of evil in the heavenly realms. Unless we as the church of Jesus Christ fight with the understanding that the victory over the devil was won by Jesus on the cross, we will not be able to take our neighborhood, our city, our country or even the ends of the world for Christ.

Jesus taught that the gates of hell would not prevail against the church. This means that the church has to come against the gates of hell, knowing that they cannot prevail. Knowing that the victory is ours, we can exercise the spiritual authority that Jesus has given to us.

Two Levels of Combat

This spiritual war has to be fought at two different

levels. We are dealing with two battlefields. The first battlefield, the smaller one, is our own life. Our combat there is against the three sources of evil—Satan, the flesh and the world. Unfortunately, many are those who have commitments to Satan. Sadly, many believers, in spite of following God's ways, don't seem to be able to free themselves from old ties. These unbroken ties are places that Satan uses to keep influencing their lives. When we turn to Jesus, we have to break away from the past and destroy every commitment and link with the enemy.

Some years ago, I ministered in Switzerland. God moved in those glorious meetings. A lady who had been involved for many years in mysticism and astrology attended one of the meetings. Though she enjoyed great social renown because of her psychic abilities, the fact is that the enemy had taken authority over her, and she was badly ill and paralyzed. The doctors couldn't find a scientific reason for her illness.

During a wonderful time of praise and worship, all by herself, without anyone's intervention, she stood up—completely recovered! She repented of her sins and was baptized. Then she shared her testimony with the whole church.

When she returned home, she filled thirty-five big bags with her books on the occult. She paid the janitor to remove those bags and burn them. Her past was behind, and she didn't want anything to do with it. Today, she is a happy woman, healthy and joyfully serving the Lord. She didn't leave any open places for Satan to return.

The second battlefield is our mission field—the area where we live, our town or city, the country to which we belong and the world that we have to reach. You may ask yourself, "What is there for me to do other than to preach the gospel?" There are many things you can do, but the most important one is to pray. The fundamental changes that our world needs have to be performed by God. That is why our praying for His mercy for our city or country is essential.

How is it possible that in a rich planet like ours, filled with an abundance of things given by God, there are still so many people in need, hungry, living in unhealthy conditions, without the essentials for leading a truly human existence?

We could probably find many political, economical and social explanations to this question. But is there a spiritual explanation? I think there is. I believe that it is pretty obvious that in our world, the devil has had ample space to do whatever he wants to do. We could very well blame political instability, bad economical administration and the new world order for increasing poverty, decreasing quality of life, unemployment and human suffering. But the truth is that the spirits of poverty, misery, exploitation, oppression and unemployment are here, on this earth. Man, even without knowing it, has given the devil the power to act.

What can we do? Who could cast out these spirits, but God's people in the name of Jesus? How will we do it? Praying, interceding, battling in prayer and doing spiritual warfare. This is our task.

PREPARING FOR BATTLE

There are valid ways in which you can prepare for battle spiritually right now. Let's take a look at some of these.

Worship the Lord.

Worshiping the Lord is the most important thing. Before being a vessel of war, the Potter made you a sanctuary vessel. Fill your mouth and your heart with praises and thanksgiving and worship the Lord. Praise and worship the Lord for what He does and who He is. Recognize His sovereignty. He is above all rulers and all powers.

Thank God for the country where you were born and where you live. If you regularly complain about your country or the city in which you live, stop right now and start to praise and worship God. Do you want a revival in your country? Do you want to overcome the powers of darkness? The way to do it, the way to get rid of darkness, is by turning on the light and establishing God's presence in the midst of our nation through our praises:

> Sing, O Daughter of Zion; shout aloud, O Israel!
> Be glad and rejoice with all your heart, O
> Daughter of Jerusalem! The LORD has taken
> away your punishment, he has turned back
> your enemy. The LORD, the King of Israel, is
> with you; never again will you fear any harm.
> —ZEPHANIAH 3:14–15

Pray and wait on the Lord.

We need to pray, cry out and listen to God. Do you know what happened after the battles of Jericho and Ai? The Israelites suffered a terrible deceit because they went ahead without waiting to hear from God. "The men of Israel sampled their provisions but did not inquire of the LORD" (Josh. 9:14). The Bible warns us against the sin of presumptuousness, the attempt to extend the kingdom of God without clear directions. After the victories at Jericho and Ai, the men of Israel were deceived by the Gibeonites because they committed the sin of not inquiring of the Lord.

Pray and listen to God's directions. Pray and intercede for your church leaders. Pray with them, and wait for God's directions for your city.

> If my people would but listen to me, if Israel
> would follow my ways, how quickly would I

subdue their enemies and turn my hand against
their foes!

—PSALM 81:13–14

Let us wait on the Lord, listen to Him and not
depend on finite understanding or human shrewdness.
The spiritual battles are won by following the Holy
Spirit's revelations.

Ask forgiveness for the sins of your city and nation.

We may believe that we do not have anything to
do with our cities' present situation. But the Word
teaches us to identify with the sins of our nation in
personal repentance. When Nehemiah prayed for
the restoration of Jerusalem, he had absolutely
nothing to do with the sins of the previous genera-
tions that had led the people into captivity. And yet
he prayed, "I confess the sins we Israelites,
including myself and my father's house, have committed against you" (Neh. 1:7). Ezra prayed the
same: "O my God, I am too ashamed and disgraced
to lift up my face to you, my God, because our sins
are higher than our heads and our guilt has reached
to the heavens" (Ezra 9:6).

They didn't pray as if they were blameless. They
identified themselves with the sins of the nation.
Perhaps you haven't murdered anyone, but you have
committed other sins that have offended God. Even

though your church may not be directly responsible for the difficult socioeconomic situation of your country, it may not have done enough for it not to happen. Ask forgiveness, not just for your society's collective sins but also for yours. Demons are not the main problem. The leading problem is the ego. Only after God has cleansed my sinful heart am I able to continue interceding.

Resist the devil.

Jesus taught us to resist the devil through fasting and prayer. You can actually have an effect on the heavenly places through prayer and fasting. Choose a day to pray and fast for your city and nation that the gospel may reach them by means of a revival.

Another way to resist the devil is with a spirit opposite to his. We overcome evil with good. If your city has a spirit of poverty, overcome the devil with your generosity. If there is a spirit of lying, overcome it with the truth. If there is a spirit of pride and arrogance, overcome it with humility.

Declare victory.

Declare and confess the Word of God, believing it in your heart. At home, every day, say in a loud voice, "God will send a revival to my city." The power of Christ is mightier than the darkness over your city. Misery and poverty will flee in the name of Jesus. Rebuke and say, "Satan, you and your demons will not possess my nation. This country belongs to Jesus Christ." Confess that the Lord will give you the victory in your church and in the plans that you have, as a congregation, to take your area and your city for Christ.

Confess Christ.

The major defeat for Satan is when you share about Christ. Ask God to give you one person this week to whom you can witness. If your prayer is sincere, if you are truly willing to do it, God will give you an opportunity to share Him with at least one person this week. The Holy Spirit will do the rest.

Work for the unity of the church.

The unity of the church is vital for spiritual warfare. Collaborate and work for the unity of the church of Jesus Christ in your city. Come together spiritually with other believers from other congregations and denominations to pray for your city and to take it spiritually. March together as God's people in Jericho, taking each area of your city in prayer. As time goes by, you will notice how the evil strongholds, the powers and the principalities in your city fall in the name of Jesus.

Appropriate the victory.

As they received the word of the Lord, the people were strengthened and encouraged:

Do not be afraid. Stand firm and you will see the deliverance the LORD will bring you today. The Egyptians you see today you will never see again. The LORD will fight for you; you need only to be still.

—EXODUS 14:13–14

If we have a simple obedience to God, the infinite God will join the finite in us. The omnipotence of God will touch our limitations. And in your city, the walls will fall down, and you will begin to see the power of God in action.

God has made us into beautiful jars that worship and enjoy communion with Him. Now the Lord is sounding the trumpet, calling us to battle. And you, sanctuary vessel, will be taken in His hands to be a jar of war. He has prepared an incredible victory for you.

A woman came with an alabaster jar of very expensive perfume, made of pure nard. She broke the jar and poured the perfume on his head.

—MARK 14:3

1 5

Alabaster Jars

GOD IS RESTORING worship in His church all over the world. He is leading us to remove man from the center of the service, placing Himself as the main recipient and crux of our meeting.

In the Bible we find a story that helps us to understand the true meaning and purpose of worship. Six days before His death, Jesus was invited to a banquet. In that house, as in any house in Israel, many different smells were noticed. Any of those present at the dinner party could smell the fragrance coming from the wheat fields. Or the smell of the sheep that were grazing nearby. Also the scent of the fig trees, the green grass and the olive trees could be noticed, along with the aroma of the food that was being prepared. But unexpectedly, a different scent filled that place. A woman had brought a pound of expensive perfume made of pure nard. She broke the jar and poured the perfume on Jesus' feet while wiping them with her hair (Luke 7:37–39).

It is very interesting to think about this scene. John is sitting and enjoying the good food. He had shook the hands of many of the guests and had hugged them also. He had seen what this woman did with that perfume and had heard Jesus' teaching. But he wasn't impressed by what he had touched, tasted, seen or heard. What impressed him and the others was what they smelled—the house was filled with the scent of the perfume. That scent of worship and praise exceeded all the other smells in the house. For an instant, for just a moment, there was only one smell—the perfume of Mary's worship.

But Judas rebuked this godly woman's attitude. He did not want that perfume to be used for worship, but given to the poor: "Why this waste of perfume? It could have been sold for more than a year's wages and the money given to the poor." For Judas and for the others, it was a waste of money. Of course, Judas belonged to another kingdom.

This story reminds me of the time when I became a Christian. God would ask me daily to surrender my life to Him. Every year He would win me over a little bit more. I knew that my consecration had to be 100 percent or nothing; therefore, I thought very carefully about my decision. The story of a young missionary named Bruce Olson had a great impact on me, and I finally recognized that as a young man I didn't have a definite purpose in life. If God wanted to use me, I was ready to surrender entirely to Him.

I was probably twenty years old when the Lord called me to the ministry. At that time I was working as a regular employee in a company. I had never been given great responsibilities, nor had I been considered for a better position. One weekend while in a Christian camp, God spoke to me: "Devote yourself exclusively to My work and nothing else." I had my own plans. I was studying then to become an engineer, but the moment God gave me a burden for the lost and invited me to surrender to His hands as His instrument, I had no doubts about what to do. I decided to quit my job the very next day to enroll in seminary.

That Monday I went to work as usual. As soon as I sat down at my desk, someone came and told me, "The general manager wants to see you." That surprised me. The general manager would always enter the building through a far away door and lock himself in his luxurious office. Why would he want to see me, a young "nobody" in his company? He had never greeted me; he was a multimillionaire too busy to even acknowledge me.

Immediately, I went to his office. As I came in, he invited me to sit down. I sunk in a huge sofa right in front of him. He said, "Sir, we have been thinking about you all weekend long. We have decided that we want you to be in charge of a new department.

You will have a unique opportunity unlike any other. We have been thinking about your talents, your future and your professional career in our company, and have decided to place you as head of the computer department. You will have a better salary, as well as receive special training."

As I was listening to this man, God was reminding me that I had renounced all that. I said, "Sir, I will be honest with you and tell you something you may not understand."

"Yes," he said, "please tell me your concerns."

So I clearly told him, "I cannot accept your offer. I'm about to enter seminary to serve God as a pastor."

Do you know the first thing he told me? "What a waste!" I identified with that woman who poured the perfume to the last drop without considering the cost. That man asked me, "How do you plan to live? What about your future, as well as your family's future?" He then started to exhort me, urging me to reconsider my decision. Of course, he couldn't understand my determination. But at least he knew that I had decided to be faithful to my calling and would not move an inch. As years went by, this businessman understood and accepted what God had done in my life. What is even more, he contributed financially to pay for seminary, delivering free food for the students. But at that initial moment, he thought it was a waste.

This is the time to surrender everything to God in worship, making a commitment to Him and to His kingdom. Many of your family members and friends will tell you, "Why do you spend so many hours in church? Why, instead of resting, do you go to preach at hospitals?" They do not understand that you have poured your whole being at the feet of Jesus. Don't expect their applause. The truly committed Christians will be criticized. We are that vessel of great value. For many, the value resides in the perfume that is stored inside. But for us, the only eternal value is in the breaking of the jar at the feet of the Master. It will be our glory. For them, it is a waste.

That was Judas's understanding as he watched Mary's surrender and adoration. But Jesus crowned her worship by saying, "Leave her alone. . . . Why are you bothering her? She has done a beautiful thing to me. The poor you will always have with you" (Mark 14:6–7).

Worship is simply repeating what Mary did. It is to prostrate ourselves before the Lord, recognizing Him as Lord. It is surrendering to Him, in an act of worship, our most valuable and costly possession—our life. As Judas, we are tempted to devote our attention, our costly perfume, our being to something else rather than to the worship of our Lord. As you read these lines, you are probably smelling many different "perfumes"— the scent of your worries, the aroma of your problems, needs and sicknesses. Therefore,

Jesus tells you, "Problems and difficulties you will always have with you; but now, let your house be filled with the sweet fragrance of your adoration."

We have already seen how the vessel of our life starts to crack and break due to sin, disobedience, dualism and negative feelings. But what a paradox we encounter in God's dynamics, in the way the Potter works in us. He says something rather strange: "The first step in restoring a broken jar is *to break it*."

That woman at Bethany broke before Jesus Christ in humility and adoration. While pride breaks our jars, she broke her jar in order to do away with pride. The Word of God says that "she poured it on Jesus' feet and wiped his feet with her hair. And the house was filled with the fragrance of the perfume" (John 12:3). This means that this woman prostrated herself at the feet of Jesus; she humbled herself before Him, recognizing His lordship and her own condition, and worshiped Him. If you don't want pride to break your life, you have to break your pride in worship.

Mary did not allow bitterness and hate to fill her soul as she experienced Judas's rejection and criticism. She did not allow resentment to take control over her, breaking her down and bringing bitterness to the house. On the contrary, she broke her inner self in worship, and that place was filled with the fragrance of the perfume.

She didn't surrender only in part. Her heart was

not divided. She knew perfectly well that Jesus required complete surrender, total worship, and she knew she was acting in harmony with that. She didn't keep anything to herself, but breaking the alabaster jar, she poured it all out. When our yielding is incomplete and we don't follow Jesus wholeheartedly, our jars break in two. But when we break the jar completely in adoration, the surrender is absolute, and the Potter rebuilds us according to His perfect plan.

This healthy breaking will enable the anointing of the Holy Spirit in us to come out and touch everything around us. We don't need anything new coming from the outside. We need to free up the anointing that is already in us. The ministries that God raises with anointing are used by Him to lead us to the most holy place of His presence. There, facing Jesus, we can be broken. Only in front of Christ can true breaking occur. It couldn't be any other way. In Him is the grace that breaks the alabaster jar, so that the precious in us can be poured out and flow according to the Potter's exact design.

The river of living waters is already in you—you don't have to depend on man! Jesus, when speaking about the Holy Spirit we would receive, said that rivers of living waters would flow from within us. The anointing is already in you. What you need is brokenness. And God is raising ministries that will help us to take that essential step of faith.

One of today's sins is the same as the one at the church at Laodicea. As I travel around the world and see the revival God is bringing, I worry about the pastors and leaders who are satisfied with things as they are. God told the church at Laodicea that He was going to spit it out of His mouth because it was lukewarm.

Why was that church lukewarm? Because it said of itself, "I am rich; I have acquired wealth and do not need a thing."

Yet God saw it as wretched, pitiful, poor, blind and naked. What a different viewpoint! The church was saying, "I'm OK."

God was saying, "I don't think so."

Let us not be satisfied; let us never lose our hunger and thirst for God and give way to conformity. Let's not be lukewarm. God wants us to look for more, and He will give us more.

You are the jar of clay that holds the excellence of God's power. Stop praying for the power and presence that is already within you. Start yielding completely, not holding anything back. Pour out your life. You have the perfume made of pure nard already in you. Be broken, and God's fragrance in you will spread and fill the place with the aroma of Jesus Christ.

If you do, everybody will know that you are a child of God. When you go into a hospital, restaurant, bank, school, university, market and work, the

1 6

Jars of Oil

GOD HAS TREMENDOUSLY blessed Betty and me during the years we have been ministering to the Lord. By His mercy, He has given us the privilege of being channels of His grace, yielded jars of clay that can pour out the great treasure of His presence and power on many others. We saw multitudes of people go from death to life in an instant as they accepted Jesus Christ as their Lord and Savior. Many who were under the devil's oppression have been set free from the darkness that held them captive and enjoy precious freedom in Christ. In each one of our crusades, God surprised us with incredible miracles of healing. All along, we have seen God's wonderful hand moving and bringing restoration, reconciliation, prosperity, growth, multiplication and all sorts of blessings.

I understand the gospel in an integral way. Therefore, I try to help each person find the answer to his or her particular need in the sweet person of Jesus Christ. But if I had to choose one element that has been, by God's will, distinctive of our ministry, it is the particular fact of having been channels of restoration and spiritual renewal to so many lives and ministries. Hundreds of thousands of people who attended our meetings in different parts of the world have testified of a fresh anointing that brought changes in their lives, in their communion with God and in their Christian service.

For example, pastors from different denominations who were frustrated with their personal lives and ministries were completely transformed along with their congregations. With God's fresh anointing they ministered in a new level of power and authority, gathering the fruit of their personal revival.

When the fresh oil of the anointing is poured out on the hearts of believers, they are forever changed. Some have never had an abiding experience with the Holy Spirit. The experience of others was dry and dormant, almost stuck because of the routine. But suddenly, like a tumultuous river, the Holy Spirit flooded their lives in a new way. Like a mighty wind, He blew over them, and they were never the same again.

No matter what their geographical context, socioeconomic reality or religious background, believers around the world enjoy the same experiences: a new communion with the Holy Spirit, a new passion to testify, a fervent desire to seek more of God, a new and incredible joy and a hunger and thirst to serve the Lord more and more.

All over the world, believers express the same interest and concern at maintaining their fresh anointing. Wherever I go I hear the same question: "Pastor Claudio, what do I do to keep the anointing flowing?" Some who are filled with the oil and burning with the fire of the Holy Spirit are afraid of losing that wonderful communion with God. For others who have enjoyed that fullness, the jar has broken and the oil has been lost on the way. So the question becomes urgent: What do I do to keep the anointing flowing?

The text at the opening of this chapter is taken from the Bible story of the encounter between Elijah and the widow at Zarephath. The widow was gathering sticks to make a fire to prepare the last meal she and her son would have, since they had nothing else to eat. After taking that last bite, they would simply prepare to die. Elijah calls her and asks for a little water in a jar so that he could have a drink and a piece of bread to eat. She explains to him that she has only a handful of flour in a jar and a little oil in a jug. When that is gone, she and her son would just die.

This describes the condition of many believers. They are God's children, and the oil of the Holy Spirit is in their lives. But their spiritual life is as good as dead—they barely have any oil in their jugs.

There is very little anointing. They have a devotional life, but it is carried out with great effort, almost as a burden. They serve the Lord, but without any anointing, without any fruit.

Many Christians, aware that their situation is like that of the widow of Zarephath, prepare themselves for their spiritual death. They resign themselves to living Christian lives without joy, power or sparkle. Like that woman, they live their faith without expectation, just waiting to die.

But she had an encounter with the anointed prophet Elijah. Elijah gave the widow a list of instructions so that the oil would not run dry. I want us to examine these instructions together.

THE CORRECT ATTITUDE

The first order that the widow received from Elijah has to do with the correct attitude. Elijah's instruction was, "Don't be afraid" (1 Kings 17:13). My first advice to you is, "Do not fear." Unfortunately, a spirit of fear holds many Christians in bondage and hinders them from living an abundant life. Often the very thing they fear eventually happens to them.

Elijah told the woman not to be afraid. She had to stop resigning herself to the fact that she and her son were going to die. She had to free her mind from negative thoughts and from unbelief. The moment some Christians have a new experience with the Lord, they start thinking, *I wonder how long this will last?* Maybe they allowed the flame of God's fire to go out and feel unqualified to start all over again. Or they may be afraid of losing the fresh anointing they have received. We cannot think this way—immersed in unbelief, doubts and fear.

When God anointed you with His Holy Spirit, He didn't give you a spirit of timidity or fear. The oil that descended upon you is the spirit of love, power and self-control (2 Tim. 1:7). Don't resign yourself to the fact that your Christian life will die a slow death. Don't accept the fact that your fellowship with God is fading. Don't accept a weak life of witnessing and service as normal. Don't be paralyzed by fear so that you end up losing all that God has given you. If you follow the instructions of the Word we are studying together, the oil of the anointing of the Holy Spirit in your life will not run dry.

THE PRIORITY IN LIFE

Elijah's second recommendation has to do with the *priorities in life.* The woman told him that she would go home to cook a meal for herself and her son with that handful of flour and oil, so that they may eat it and then die. Elijah makes an interesting request. He says, "Go home and do as you have said. But *first* make a small cake of bread for me from what you have and bring it to me, and then make something for yourself and your son" (1 Kings 17:13, emphasis added). The word *first* is a key word. At first glance, we would think that Elijah is an insensitive man. Although he knew that this was an extremely poor widow who only had a few bites to eat before she died of hunger, he still asks her to provide some food for him to eat. But it is not so. Elijah is applying a basic principle for receiving God's blessing.

This principle applies to our finances, as in the widow's situation, but it also applies to everything else. Do you want blessings in your family life, your studies, your vocation, your profession, your relationships and your ministry? Apply this principle then. It is the priorities principle. Give first to God; God, who doesn't owe anybody anything, will give you what you need and even more. Consecrate your life to God. Let Him be the most important thing in your life. If you do, the oil of the anointing of the Holy Spirit will not run dry. I have ministered to thousands and thousands of people, and I have never known anyone who, having put Jesus first in his or her life, has ever lost the intensity of the anointing.

THE REQUIRED OBEDIENCE

The third precept to take into account for the spiritual oil not to run dry is that of *obedience*. Just for a moment, try to place yourself in that widow's situation. You are in the midst of a catastrophic national crisis. Because of a drought, there is absolutely no food. All you have left is a handful of flour and a little oil in your jug. All you can do is eat and then die. But suddenly, someone appears and tells you, "Before you and your son get to eat, give me something to eat." What would you have done, and what would you have said?

When the Potter places His hands on you and molds you as His jar, He fills you with oil so that you can be a blessing to others. It is disobedience that ruins the jar and causes the oil to spill. Many believers are greatly anointed by God to minister powerfully with signs and wonders. God commands them to pray for the sick in His name, for He will heal them. But in spite of the anointing, when they are in front of a person who is sick, instead of following God's instructions, they become afraid, lose their faith and end up disobeying. They do this over and over again until God cannot trust them any longer. And so, very slowly, the anointing decreases.

Many believers have received a wonderful anointing from God. He touches them, fills them with joy, gives them external evidences so they learn to trust and fills them to overflowing with His love. Happily, they receive this anointing but continue with sin in their lives. They want the anointing of power, but they are not willing to abandon those things that come against Him who gives the anointing. Anointing and sin can't walk together too far. Either the anointing gets rid of the sin, or the sin gets rid of the anointing, because darkness has no fellowship with light. Disobedience breaks the jar and spoils the oil of the anointing. It is important to live a life of obedience so that the oil will not run dry.

THE NECESSARY SOLITUDE

Elijah tells the widow to go home. God was going to do an amazing thing in her life, and she needed to be at home. The believer has to understand once again the importance of time alone with God. In the last years we have seen many people searching for God. Church services are filled with people who praise God and want to be ministered to. This is wonderful, but it has to be in conjunction with our private time with God.

Our anointing for public ministry corresponds directly to the time we spend alone with God. There are no secrets. Anointed men who have been raised up by God in each generation have been men whose prayer lives were rich and consistent. Prayer must be a daily practice for every believer. In addition to our daily quiet time with God, it is important to be alone with Him as much as possible—not only to seek more of Him, but also for our anointing to increase. It is a type of personal retreat. We see Jesus practicing this in His own life, pulling away to be alone with His Father. It was the space He created to receive more holy anointing from His Father.

THE SHARED ANOINTING

Elijah and Elisha not only had similar names; they also had similar ministries. In 2 Kings Elisha performs a similar miracle of provision for another widow. In this case, it is a prophet's widow. Her husband had revered God, but he had died, and there were debts to pay. Since she didn't have the means to pay, the creditor wanted to take her two sons as his slaves. Elisha asked the widow what she had in her house. She answered, "Your servant has nothing there at all, except a little oil."

It doesn't matter what your need may be—financial, emotional, relational, familial, occupational or ministerial. If there is oil in the jar, God will change your need into a blessing.

Elisha tells the widow what to do with that jar of oil. But similar to the story of Elijah and the widow of Zarephtah, what the prophet tells this widow sounds strange and a bit ridiculous: "Go around and ask all your neighbors for empty jars. Don't ask for just a few. Then go inside and shut the door behind you and your sons. Pour oil into all the jars, and as each is filled, put it to one side" (2 Kings 4:3–4).

Don't you think this sounds a bit foolish? Asking the neighbors for oil instead of jars would make a little bit more sense to me. The oil was valuable and negotiable, and then they could have money to pay the creditor. The jars had very little value. She should ask for oil, not for jars. But Elisha orders her to ask for jars! The teaching is pretty obvious. For the anointing not to run dry, we have to share it. Many believers should learn this truth. They spend their time praying for more anointing, more oil. But God is telling them, "Don't ask for oil; ask for more jars. If there are more jars, I will pour more oil, and the oil of my anointing will never cease."

The Word says that the jars were filled with oil. The sons kept bringing more jars, and instead of running dry, the oil kept on flowing, filling more and more jars. It finally ceased to flow when there were no more jars to fill. The oil of the anointing will cease when you stop having other jars with which to share your blessings. As long as there are new jars to hold the Holy Spirit's oil, the anointing will go on.

The widow and her sons had to go to their neighbors looking for jars. You are the jar that is full of oil. Your neighbors, family members, friends and the people around you are the jars with which you want to share Calvary's work. As long as you speak to them about the Lord, serve them, share your anointing with them, your oil will stay fresh and intact.

The people who share their lives with you—at home, at work, in the neighborhood, in your school—are empty jars. They are jars, because the Potter also created them as He created you. But they are empty; they don't have the oil of the presence of the Holy Spirit. They are empty vessels, needy, lacking all those things that only Jesus Christ can produce in people's lives. When you bless them, two things happen. They will not be empty anymore, and your oil won't run dry but will continue to flow even more.

God wants to bring about the last great move of His Holy Spirit on all flesh. Being a blessing to those around you is only the beginning—He expects that. Directly or indirectly, He wants your influence to reach to the ends of the world. God is encouraging His church to a greater commitment to missions. We must pray for the outpouring of the Holy Spirit over every people, race, tongue and nation, so that a powerful revival can cover the whole face of the earth.

The jars the widow had to request had several characteristics. They had to be borrowed from the neighbors; they had to be empty; and they had to be "not just a few" (v. 3). I want you to know that if you ask for jars and not only oil, God will send you a lot of people in need so that you can minister and bless them. All of a sudden you will start seeing people in a new way. You will not look at them in a superficial way, but the Holy Spirit will start to show you the needs that lie deep in their hearts. You will be able to minister to them in a specific way, and the anointing will go with you and will increase in you. Never forget that the only time the oil runs dry is when there are no more vessels to fill.

The Potter formed you and made you into a jar. When you are filled with the oil of the Spirit, you bless those around you. If you are feeling as hopeless as the widow of Zarephath, I want to encourage you not to allow your spiritual life to die, but to be open to receive a new anointing.

If you have asked for oil, you have received God's anointing already. Now ask for jars, and share with them the oil with which God has filled you.

And whenever you are thirsty, go and get a drink from the water jars the men have filled.

—R<small>UTH</small> 2:9

Jars of Water

COULD GOD BE extending the same invitation as Boaz made to Ruth to people in need? Could God be telling those who don't have Christ in their lives, who are empty, depressed, grieved, sick and oppressed, to go and get a drink from the water jars the servants, the Christians, have filled? Would the people who are in need find in you, a jar of the Lord, a true answer to their lives—the fresh water that quenches their thirst? Are you a servant who can provide water to the thirsty and bless those in need?

Nine centuries after Ruth's story, another similar episode took place. Just like Ruth the Moabite, the protagonist was a thirsty foreigner. Her story is found in the Gospel of John, chapter 4. Even though we don't know her name, today she is known as the Samaritan woman.

This episode in the life and ministry of Jesus gives

us a chance to understand God's great love for us. Do you know that your life is extremely valuable to God? He wants the whole world to know Jesus as its Lord and Savior.

Let us consider carefully this story. The first thirty verses in this chapter are devoted to the way in which Jesus relates to a Samaritan woman. Only three verses are devoted to the revival in Samaria.

We would have dedicated whole pages to what God did in a city, and then, almost casually, as a mere example, we would have shared a personal experience. But God does things differently. Of course He was interested in Samaria's revival, but the woman interested Him more. First of all, because He loved her and valued her as an individual. Second, because He knew that if He paid attention to that woman of easy virtue, without any religious merit, it would bring revival to the whole town. God is interested in your city's revival. But before that, and in order for it to take place, *He has to deal with you first.*

Jesus was tired, hungry and thirsty, but this woman's need came first: "My food...is to do the will of him who sent me and to finish his work" (John 4:34). The most important thing for the Lord was not to satisfy His own desires and needs, but to fulfill the mission that the Father had entrusted to Him when He sent Him into this world. That mission was to meet people's needs. Jesus was not satisfied with a partial fulfillment of that mission. He wanted to complete it. He wanted everybody to have a chance to live an eternal life, full of God's purposes. That was the will that the Father had revealed to Him, and He, as the beloved Son, wanted to obey it. God hasn't changed. His heart still cries out today for the unsaved.

God is interested in what goes on here on earth. The knowledge of His glory is to be revealed on earth, and He needs you for that. Just as the Samaritan woman was the vehicle He used to reach a whole town, He wants to use you to reach your city and nation. Because He loves you and loves your people, His eyes are set on you.

You may believe that in order for revival to occur, you must reach a multitude of people. But that is not what happened in this story in chapter 4 of the Gospel of John. Jesus didn't start by ministering to a multitude of Samaritans. He started by meeting the needs of one person, one woman, with a bad reputation. Understand this story, and watch what Jesus did, because that is the way God intends to use you. Don't think about a multitude; think of just one person. The multiplication will follow, because it is God who does the work.

OVERCOMING RACIAL BARRIERS

Jesus was interested in the Samaritan woman. But

confrontation didn't come easily—Jesus had to break down many barriers. The first was the racial barrier. Jews and Samaritans were not on speaking terms. They were enemies. The Jews considered the Samaritans impure. At a earlier time in history, the Samaritans had intermingled with foreigners and were forever branded as impure. That is why a Jew would never have a relationship with a Samaritan. Likewise, the Samaritans would not forgive the Jews for the destruction of their temple at Gerizim. They were avowed enemies.

However, Jesus did not perceive that woman as an enemy. He saw a woman who needed to be blessed, one who was capable of passing that blessing on to others. Remember that when God found you, you were His enemy. The Bible says that when we are not yielded to His will, we live as God's enemies. Yet God didn't see you as His enemy, but rather as someone in need of His love. And He didn't just see you, but all those who would some day be touched by your ministry. Jesus didn't stop to examine the quarrels and human differences.

There will always be people who have racial, political, economical or other differences with you. The Lord wants you to see them just as He sees them—people who need His touch and who are future multipliers of the blessing. They are the vehicles of the revival, and so are you.

OVERCOMING SOCIAL BARRIERS

Jesus also had to overcome social barriers. In those days a man would not talk to a woman in public. And yet Jesus was ready to overcome all prejudice to minister to a very unhappy woman who had no peace.

He's not interested in prejudices or religious matters. He is only interested in people. The Samaritan woman worshiped in Mount Gerizim and the Jews in Jerusalem. Jesus didn't care about that. He is not interested in your religion—He's interested in your life. Jesus overcame religious and social prejudices to bring abundant, eternal life to everyone.

He wants you to be willing to overcome all social and personal prejudices in your life. He wants to reach the depths of a person, the place where their true situation is revealed. There the sharp pain of loneliness is felt, the bitterness of disdain is tasted. There they feel abandonment and lack of love. There the beating of their wounded heart is heard and persistent anguish lingers, taking peace away and manifesting unhappiness. That is where the Lord needs you. He wants to reach that deep place in people and bring radical change to them.

OVERCOMING SPIRITUAL BARRIERS

In order to be a blessing to the Samaritan woman, and

through her to bless a whole town, Jesus had to overcome some spiritual barriers. Jesus Christ, the Son of God who had no sin, met this woman of dubious reputation—a miracle of love. God, the three times holy, hates sin, yet wants to have intimate fellowship with each one of us. He hates sin because sin separates us from Him and destroys our relationship with Him and with others.

Jesus didn't beat around the bush. He went straight to the point: "You are right when you say you have no husband. The fact is, you have had five husbands, and the man you now have is not your husband" (John 4:17–18). Jesus doesn't want to hide our sins or pretend that they are not there. He knows perfectly well that as long as we are in bondage to sin we can't be happy. He demands true repentance and a complete surrender to Him. As He has dealt with you, He wants you to lead others to repentance and to the surrender of their hearts to Christ.

THERE IS AN EASY METHOD

His method to reach the Samaritan woman was quite simple. It is an example for us to follow. Let us see some of its aspects.

Establish contact.

The first thing He did was to establish contact with

her. Some of the best opportunities to evangelize take place naturally, amidst normal circumstances—at work, at home, at the bus stop, during a taxi drive, standing in line at the bank or the supermarket or having a cup of coffee with a friend.

Opportunities are there if we are open to them. If we are not willing to share our faith with others, we will always find excuses not to do it. But if we fervently desire that others may know Jesus Christ, we will always find opportunities to share our faith, and the Holy Spirit will do the rest.

People are hungry for God. They are expressing their needs as never before. Without realizing it, they are crying out for a deeper relationship with us. They may not say it, but they are begging us to listen to their problems. Through their attitudes, they reveal how much they need our love and our peace. In other words, they are asking us to preach Jesus to them.

Our world is ready, like never before, to receive Christ. Some people in the church may say, "What revival are you talking about? Don't you see where the world is going? We are still far away from a revival." Jesus' disciples thought this way, and so He had to correct their vision: "Do you not say, 'Four months more and then the harvest'? I tell you, open your eyes and look at the fields! They are ripe for harvest" (John 4:35). Jesus is telling us still that the fields are ripe for harvest.

Like the Samaritan woman, some people may

appear to have no perceivable needs. But Jesus looked deep inside of her. Outside appearances can be very deceiving. People may not want to admit it, but their hearts are empty. The only person who can dwell in their hearts and give meaning to their lives is our Lord Jesus Christ. Just as denying the existence of food fails to remove hunger because man was created to be physically nourished, so denying the existence of God will fail to remove spiritual hunger because man was created to live in harmony with our Creator.

Pray that God will give you the opportunity to share the gospel today and every day. Seek that personal encounter in prayer, and God will open the door for you. He will give you discernment for the person's real need, and will also give you the words and the power to touch each person with His infinite love.

Awaken the person's attention.

Jesus awakened the woman's curiosity by confronting her with her reality. Her life was lacking something. She experienced no satisfaction. She felt empty, dry, disillusioned and depressed.

How can you get people's attention? You do so with a life that is different—not only because of *what you do,* but because of *what you are* and *what you may become.* A joyful, peaceful and secure life will trigger their curiosity for more. People don't want words; they want to see changed lives. You don't have to be a preacher; just tell them what Christ has done in your life and show them the evidence of this change in your actions.

Respond to their needs.

Jesus specifically addressed the person's need. The Samaritan woman tried to change the subject by asking Him where she should worship. Jesus responded to her question kindly, but quickly returned to her spiritual problem.

If you want your testimony to be effective, it has to respond to the person's specific needs. The gospel is not an impersonal presentation—it is effective when it responds to the needs of the person in front of you. When Jesus sent the seventy on a mission, He first told them to heal the sick. Only then were they to preach the gospel of the kingdom. We confront people with the Good News of Jesus Christ through each person's needs.

Lead them to make a decision.

Jesus led the Samaritan woman to surrender herself. The woman told Him, "I know that Messiah (called Christ) is coming. When he comes, he will explain everything to us" (John 4:25). In other words, what she said was, "Everything You are telling me is very interesting, but as for right now there is nothing we can do."

But Jesus confronted her by saying, "I who speak

to you am he" (v. 26).

Every time the gospel is presented is a critical moment. With gentleness and care, we need to lead people to make a decision. Don't hinder them with fears or extreme caution. Once a person hears your testimony and understands how Jesus responds to personal needs, simply ask, "Would you like me to lead you in a personal prayer so that you can receive Jesus Christ as your Lord?"

As you can see, the method is simple. Pray for the opportunity; establish personal contact; be interested in the other person's needs; share your testimony in response to that need; and finally, lead that person to receive Christ as Lord of his or her life.

Jars Transformed Into Springs of Water

The main concern is not how to do it. As we have seen, that is quite simple. The most important thing is not to make the mistake common among Christians of thinking erroneously that evangelizing is only done by extraordinary people—pastors, missionaries, ministers, deacons or elders. God doesn't need any extraordinary people. He needs ordinary people to manifest the love and the power of an extraordinary God.

The Samaritan woman came to Jacob's well with a jar in her hand to get some water for herself. But when she met Jesus, He changed that jar into springs of water. She had to decide that the water was not only for herself, but it was a spring of water welling up within her to bring eternal life to others.

You must choose between being a jar that gathers water for yourself alone or a fountain of water welling up into eternal life for others. In reality, we don't have an option. We have been called to be fountains. God called you to be a blessing to others. A self-centered Christian is a contradiction in terms. One cannot be a Christian while living for oneself. Are we going to be jars, concerned about ourselves alone, always hoping to receive? Are we going to be jars that do not share the gospel because of our concern of what others may think, indifferent to other people's needs or simply thinking that God rescued us to do as we wish? On the contrary, God called us to be springs of water, authentic Christians. Our center is now Christ. Our minds are not ours but the mind of Christ, with His thoughts and His love for others.

Allow God to use this book to change the direction of your life. He made you a jar, so that you can receive all His love and power. But now, God wants you to become a fountain of water. As you finish this chapter, don't just say, "Lord, bless me." Let your cry be, "Lord, help me to be a blessing to others."

"Bring me a new bowl," he said, "and put salt in it." So they brought it to him. Then he went out to the spring and threw the salt into it, saying, "This is what the LORD says: 'I have healed this water. Never again will it cause death or make the land unproductive.'"

—2 KINGS 2:20–21

Jars of Salt

ONE OF THE imperatives that is becoming more evident every day in relationship to the church's mission in today's world is that of taking our cities for Christ and placing them under God's kingdom. During most of our history, we have considered this as an almost impossible task. However, many prophetic voices today are encouraging us to take our cities for the Lord.

When God sent specific messages to the seven churches in Asia Minor through His servant John, He closed each one with the admonition to hear what the Holy Spirit was saying to the churches (Rev. 2–3). That same exhortation is valid today. Each generation of believers has to pay attention and listen to the emphasis that the Holy Spirit places on the church in a specific period of its history.

The Lord's mandate to Jonah to win a huge city

for Him seems to be the mandate for today. The divine order to Jonah was very clear: "Go to the great city of Nineveh and proclaim to it the message I give you" (Jon. 3:2). The Lord sent him to that big city to proclaim His message.

Today, at the end of the twentieth century, and soon before the coming of Jesus Christ in all His glory, the Holy Spirit is giving the same command given to Jonah: "Go to the great city of Nineveh and proclaim to it the message I give you."

The imperative to reach our city for Christ is based on three fundamental principles: first, God is interested in our cities; second, God is sending us to the cities; and third, God wants to save the cities. Let us examine each principle carefully.

GOD IS INTERESTED IN OUR CITIES

Cities occupy an important place in God's redemptive strategy. God's purpose is that all men may be saved:

> I urge, then, first of all, that requests, prayers, intercession and thanksgiving be made for everyone—for kings and all those in authority, that we may live peaceful and quiet lives in all godliness and holiness. This is good, and pleases God our Savior, who wants all men to be saved

and to come to a knowledge of the truth.

—1 TIMOTHY 2:1–4

As you can see, Christ's redeeming work is not selective, but rather, it hopes to reach all sinners:

> For there is one God and one mediator between God and men, the man Christ Jesus, who gave himself as a ransom for all men—the testimony given in its proper time.
>
> —1 TIMOTHY 2:5–6

God's patience in delaying His return responds to His desire to give all men an opportunity to repent. He does not want anyone to perish and be eternally condemned: "The Lord is not slow in keeping his promise, as some understand slowness. He is patient with you, not wanting anyone to perish, but everyone to come to repentance" (2 Pet. 3:9).

God considers the preaching of the message of redemption in the cities to be extremely important. It is there that the highest concentration of people in need of salvation is found.

Cities are important to God. In the Old Testament, we see how God sent messengers like Jonah to call entire cities to repentance. In the New Testament, we find Jesus crying for the city of Jerusalem: "O Jerusalem, Jerusalem, you who kill the prophets and stone those sent to you, how often I have longed to gather your children together, as a hen gathers her chicks under her wings, but you were not willing!" (Luke 13:34).

For the same reasons, the devil is extremely interested in our cities. It is not a coincidence that in the Book of Revelation, the final battle between God and Satan is centered on two cities—Jerusalem and Babylon. As someone once said, "The history of salvation started in a garden, the Garden of Eden, and will finish in a city, the New Jerusalem."

GOD SENDS US TO THE CITIES

The Great Commission Jesus gave to the church began in a city, Jerusalem, and it will have its culmination, as we already saw, in another city, the New Jerusalem. This will be God's eternal dwelling with His people. In a time when most of the people lived in rural areas, Jesus chose a city as the starting point for His disciples' mission.

Jesus told them to stay in the city and wait for the power from above to come upon them. Then they had to take the city for Him. Acts 1:8 implies that they were not supposed to move on to Judea and Samaria until Jerusalem was completely evangelized. Human reasoning would have followed a completely different strategy: from the ends of the world to Jerusalem. None of us would have chosen Jerusalem to start a new religious group, especially

Christianity. That city's life rotated around a well-established religion, Judaism. There were the priests, the temple and the highest concentration of ritual and worship in the entire nation.

Besides, only a few days had gone by since Jesus had been judged by the authorities, condemned, publicly crucified and buried—in Jerusalem. The atmosphere wasn't exactly the best to initiate any evangelistic activity in that city. We would not have chosen that strategy. But Jesus did.

And He not only chose Jerusalem, but He also chose men who did not belong to that city to take it. His disciples had absolutely no urban experience. They didn't have a network of contacts or any social, economical or political relationships in Jerusalem to contribute to the evangelistic mission that Jesus had entrusted to them. On the contrary, the disciples were men from various towns of Galilee. In the Gospel of John, we can appreciate the social prejudice that the people had against those small towns: "Nazareth! Can anything good come from there?" The "establishment" despised the workers chosen by Jesus to reach the city of Jerusalem as ignorant and primitive.

In spite of this, the Great Commission was fulfilled in a city like Jerusalem. A few weeks after Jesus' departure, Jerusalem was saturated with the gospel. When Peter and John were persecuted and presented before the Sanhedrin, there the high priest exhorted them, saying, "We gave you strict orders not to teach in this name...yet you have filled Jerusalem with your teaching and are determined to make us guilty of this man's blood" (Acts 5:28).

A few days later, the church left the upper room, and, filled with the Holy Spirit, they saturated the streets of the city with the gospel of Jesus Christ. They clearly understood that the anointing they had received from the Holy Spirit was not so they could hold beautiful services in the upper room. God had filled them with His Spirit so they would, in turn, fill the city with His presence.

But the spiritual avalanche didn't stop at the gates of Jerusalem. It went on to Samaria and then Antioch. There in Antioch, the same thing happened all over again. Whole crowds were won over to Christ: "The Lord's hand was with them, and a great number of people believed and turned to the Lord." When those in Jerusalem found out what was going on in Antioch, they sent Barnabas. Through Barnabas' ministry "a great number of people were brought to the Lord." (See Acts 11:19–26.) This is how the first Gentile church—a city-church—was formed.

The same thing would happen later on in Ephesus. The first of Paul's visits was short. (See Acts 18:19–21.) In the second one, Paul met a group of twelve believers, and they formed a church. Ephesus was a city under the dominion of organized religion. Its entire social and economical life centered on the worship of Diana. On top of this, the local synagogue openly opposed Paul (Acts 19:9). However, in spite of all this, for two years the city of Ephesus listened to the gospel. And from that city, the gospel saturated the entire region: "This went on for two years, so that all the Jews and Greeks who lived in the province of Asia heard the word of the Lord" (Acts 19:10). When Paul finally left Asia Minor, he could say to the church in Rome, "But now that there is no more place for me to work in these regions..." (Rom. 15:23).

GOD WANTS TO USE YOU TO HELP TO SAVE CITIES

If God is going to use you to reach your city for Christ, it will be necessary to do it through powerful evangelism, supported by an equally powerful prayer life.

It will be necessary to deliver a committed verbal testimony of the gospel. That is the way it was in Jerusalem. The Word declares, "All of them were filled with the Holy Spirit and began to speak in other tongues as the Spirit enabled them" (Acts 2:4). The outcome was that about three thousand were added to their number that day (Acts 2:41).

In spite of opposition and even persecution, they were committed to evangelize.

"Now, Lord, consider their threats and enable

your servants to speak your word with great
boldness. Stretch out your hand to heal and
perform miraculous signs and wonders through
the name of your holy servant Jesus." After they
prayed, the place where they were meeting was
shaken. And they were all filled with the Holy
Spirit and spoke the word of God boldly.

—ACTS 4:29–31

Something similar occurred at the city of Antioch.
Some believers from Cyprus and Cyrene could not
contain themselves and spoke to the Greeks, and a
great number of them believed and gave their lives to
the Lord (Acts 11:20–21).

For your city to be taken over by the gospel, you
will need an attitude of determination and commitment. No matter the circumstances or the
opposition, God wants you to preach the Word of
God boldly. Undoubtedly, it is important for signs of
God's mighty works to accompany the words. For a
city to be shaken by the gospel, it is of major importance that a gospel of power be manifested.

The gospel of power was manifested in the city of
Jerusalem. That city had risen up to kill Jesus; its religious life revolved around Judaism. And yet, in a few
weeks, it was saturated by the gospel, and thousands
upon thousands gave their lives to the Lord. They
could not deny the signs and wonders that took place
in the name of Jesus Christ. People were "utterly

amazed... everyone was filled with awe, and many wonders and miraculous signs were done by the apostles" (Acts 2:7, 43).

Of course they were amazed, considering that "the apostles performed many miraculous signs and wonders among the people.... People brought the sick into the streets and laid them on beds and mats so that at least Peter's shadow might fall on some of them as he passed by. Crowds gathered also from the towns around Jerusalem, bringing their sick and those tormented by evil spirits, and all of them were healed" (Acts 5:12, 15–16). Your city will be impacted when they not only hear your bold preaching, but also witness the accompanying signs that confirm it.

Signs and wonders followed the preaching of the word in Antioch: "The Lord's hand was with them, and a great number of people believed and turned to the Lord" (Acts 11:21). The same took place in the city of Ephesus: "God did extraordinary miracles through Paul, so that even handkerchiefs and aprons that had touched him were taken to the sick, and their illnesses were cured and the evil spirits left them" (Acts 19:11–12).

PRAYER—THE KEY TO THE CITY

Intercessory prayer was the key to the conversions in Jerusalem. The church was in prayer constantly.

They devoted themselves to prayer (Acts 2:42). Prayer was not limited to prayer meetings or to a series of vigils or special programs. Prayer was their lifestyle.

Prayer wasn't only a means of communicating with God—it was a tool for evangelization. It was the way to witness and reach the city. As they prayed for the people, God would back them up with signs and wonders. Consequently, the people's receptivity was great, and many turned to the Lord and joined the church.

Many wonderful things are taking place right now in cities. Paul, in his first letter to Timothy, tells us how to reach our cities through prayer that gives rise to God's miracles and opens the door to the gospel.

- Pray for everyone in a city: "I urge, then, first of all, that requests, prayers, intercession and thanksgiving be made for everyone" (1 Tim. 2:1).

- Pray for the authorities and those in key positions in the city: "...for kings and all those in authority" (1 Tim. 2:2).

- Pray that all may be saved: We have to be in harmony with God's will, "who wants all men to be saved and to come to a knowledge of the truth" (1 Tim. 2:4).

- Pray where the people are: "I want men every-where to lift up holy hands in prayer" (1 Tim. 2:8).

For a number of years, the church has been hidden, and the cities have been sinking in dark-ness. But when the church rises and shines, everything changes. The next day after one of our crusades in Spain, somebody knocked at the door of the pastor's house and said, "I have been living here for years, and I had never seen this church." How incredible!

We need to be jars of salt. The text at the beginning of this chapter takes place in an urban context: "The men of the city said to Elisha, 'Look, our lord, this town is well situated, as you can see, but the water is bad and the land is unproductive" (2 Kings 2:19). They could recognize that the city of Jericho's nat-ural conditions were good, but there was something that made the whole area unproductive. Because they loved their city, they asked God's servant for help. The reason God cannot use many Christians to bless their cities is because they don't love the place where God has put them. They are always com-plaining about pollution, traffic, the climate, overpopulation and many other things. God will not be able to use us if we don't love our cities first.

Given the fact that the city of Jericho was close to the Dead Sea, its waters were salty and sulfurous.

The water was not adequate for watering or for drinking. So Elisha gave the men an order:

> "Bring me a new bowl," he said, "and put salt in it." So they brought it to him. Then he went out to the spring and threw the salt into it, saying, "This is what the LORD says: 'I have healed this water. Never again will it cause death or make the land unproductive.'"
>
> —2 KINGS 2:20–21

No doubt your city has many problems and sins. Your city has waters of death and sickness. Your city can only be healed through the gospel of Jesus Christ. For that to happen, God has to be able to use jars of salt.

Jesus taught us that we are the salt of the earth. But if the salt loses its saltiness, it is no longer good for anything, except to be thrown out and trampled by men (Matt. 5:13). We are jars of salt meant to heal the land. The Potter has made you a jar of salt to heal your city. He wants to use you so that one day, when talking about your city, you will be able to say, "Never again will it cause death or make the land unproductive." May God allow that to happen very soon.

...in order that He might make known the riches of His glory upon vessels of mercy, which He prepared beforehand for glory.

—ROMANS 9:23, NAS

1 9

Jars of Glory

WE ARE ENTERING a new decade, a new century—
a new millennium. We ought to have a clear vision of
the world to take for Jesus Christ. God wants to
make known the riches of His glory over all the
earth and has decided to use you and me, simple
jars of clay, to be His jars of mercy in this world.

Our society is filled with all kinds of evils. A significant part of the world's population suffers hunger and
lacks the most basic things. In spite of the world relief
organizations' struggle to bring awareness of these
kinds of needs, and their efforts to introduce a
change, our planet continues to be abused. Violence,
death, injustice and corruption are everyday things.
Technology, with all its benefits and comforts, has not
helped to resolve many of the most basic problems,
and it does not offer a satisfactory answer to men's
spiritual needs. For this very reason, many go to the

occult and satanic cults hoping to find an answer to their dissatisfaction.

Man without God is in a free fall. Ethical, racial, religious and familial problems, plus inner conflict, make us cry out for change. The church has a chance to make it happen. God is able to turn around this situation, but He is waiting for us, His church, to assume once and for all the power and the authority that He has given us. We have to wake up and proclaim the powerful gospel of Jesus Christ. We are on the eve of a great world revival. The devil knows it and is trying to bring confusion, division and distraction in order to prevent such a move of the Holy Spirit. This is the time to reflect seriously on the Great Commission, and God will do His part and pour out His great revival. The riches of His glory will be known all over the earth!

A POWERFUL PRAYER

There is a common denominator in the history of revivals: The church returns to prayer. Berridge used to say, "Every revival starts in the secret place; no heart burns in faith without secret conversations with God, and nothing can take its place." Matthew Henry pointed out: "When God is about to do an act of great mercy for His people, the first thing He will do is invite them to pray." Dear friend, God is extending to you an invitation.

He is inviting you to pray for revival.

God wants to pour a revival over us that will reach the whole world, but He needs us to pray for this to happen, just as Habakkuk did. There will be no revival without prayer.

Someone has said rightly that prayer has been the church's Cinderella. There are people interested in all of the church's activities. But whenever there is a prayer meeting, we say, "Today I'm not going to church; it's only a prayer meeting." Thank God, this has been changing in the last few years due to the move of the Holy Spirit, but we still have a long way to go.

God asks us to pray for the revival of His work. It is all right to present to God our needs; we should not stop doing that. He says in His Word, "Present your requests to God" (Phil. 4:6). But when was the last time you prayed for a revival of God's work?

Habakkuk presented his needs and those of his people before God, but he didn't stop there. He prayed:

> LORD, I have heard of your fame; I stand in awe
> of your deeds, O LORD. Renew them in our day,
> in our time make them known.
> —HABAKKUK 3:2

Can you imagine what God will do in response to His children's prayers? Are you aware of the power that will be unleashed if children, youth and adults begin to pray for revival?

The prophet cries out in his time for a revival of God's deeds. What was Israel's situation in those days? They were days of destruction, iniquity and violence. They were moments of great corruption, injustice, greed, oppression and idolatry. It is there, in the midst of a dramatic situation, that Habakkuk asks the Lord to revive His deeds.

Our situation is very similar to that one. Probably more than ever in the history of humanity we see those same signs as proof that human evil has increased. Christians can take different positions or stances. The first option is *resignation*. We say, "This is getting worse; there is no solution to it. There is nothing we can do." Skepticism and hopelessness start to rule our lives. That is how Habakkuk started: "How long, O LORD, must I call for help, but you do not listen? Or cry out to you, 'Violence!' but you do not save?" (Hab. 1:2).

Another possibility is to *complain*. Habakkuk was also familiar with this attitude: "Why do you make me look at injustice? Why do you tolerate wrong?" (1:3). But let us agree neither of these two alternatives is the right one. Resignation and complaint are not adequate to change our world's condition.

Habakkuk finally assumes the right path: Pray for God to produce the change; pray for God to revive His work in His time.

In the New American Standard it says, "Revive Thy work in the midst of the years, in the midst of the years make it known" (3:2). Let this be our prayer today. Resignation is the prayer of defeat and hopelessness. Complaint is the desperate cry of impotence. But God's people are not defeated, conquered or powerless. God's people have an extraordinary resource in times of need: prayer for the revival of God's work.

The Bible teaches us that the triumphant return of Jesus Christ, His Second Coming, will be very different from the first one. He will come riding a white horse ready to judge. He will no longer be emptied of His heavenly glory, but robed in splendor and glory. He will not come as a servant, but as a King. He will not be born in a manger, but will have authority and might. He will not come to die on a cross, but He will come to judge the world.

This idolatrous world, corrupt and full of oppression, violence and sin, will be judged, weighed and found wanting. But Habakkuk's prayer, as well as ours, is: "Lord, in wrath remember mercy. Before expressing the final punishment, Your final wrath, remember mercy, O God. Before judgment, send a great revival to all men."

As we contemplate the current world situation, let us not get discouraged or complain. God ordains us to pray this powerful prayer: "O Lord, revive Your work in our day, O God. Perform now, in our lives, Your great deeds of the past."

A POWERFUL TESTIMONY

Divine action is the answer to prayer. If you want to know what God is about to do, you need to observe what He has done in the past. What are the great deeds of the past? No doubt about it, the list would be endless. Habakkuk reminds us of some of those great works of God in the past.

- The prophet remembers the miracles God performed in Egypt: "Plague went before him; pestilence followed his steps" (3:5).

- He remembers the dividing of the Red Sea: "Were you angry with the rivers, O LORD? Was your wrath against the streams? Did you rage against the sea...?" (v. 8). The Egyptians drowned in that sea. It is a memory, not an allegory of deliverance. It was a real and powerful deed. God opened that sea and drowned those who opposed His people.

- He remembers the crossing of the river Jordan: "Were you angry with the rivers, O LORD? Was your wrath against the streams?" (v. 8). If the crossing of the Red Sea is the memory of deliverance, the crossing of the river Jordan is the fulfillment of that liberation, the entering into the Promised Land.

• He remembers that incredible act of God in the midst of His people when God made the sun and the moon stand still: "Sun and moon stood still in the heavens" (v. 11). It was when Joshua said to the Lord in the presence of Israel: "'O sun, stand still over Gibeon, O moon, over the Valley of Aijalon.' So the sun stood still, and the moon stopped, till the nation avenged itself on its enemies, as it is written in the Book of Jashar. The sun stopped in the middle of the sky and delayed going down about a full day. There has never been a day when the LORD listened to a man. Surely the LORD was fighting for Israel!" (Josh. 10:12–14).

In times of need we are encouraged to look ahead as we remember God's deeds in the past. We remember His works of deliverance, of salvation, of splendor and of glory.

A POWERFUL OUTCOME

When we pray for revival, we rely on God's promises. He promises us that the whole earth will be filled with the knowledge of His glory, as the waters cover the sea (Hab. 2:14). He assures us that His glory covers the heavens, and His praise fills the earth (3:3). He promises us that His splendor is like the sunrise, and that rays flash from His hand, which show the power that is hidden in Him (3:4).

When we pray to the Lord for revival, we know that our prayer has already been answered. When we pray according to God's will, as it says in His Word, we can be sure that our prayer will be answered. God tells us to pray for revival simply because He wants to send revival.

Would you like to know what is going to happen? As in the past, God will bring a revival where the Word will be followed by great miracles. As the signs that were performed in Egypt, God will endorse our words with powerful deeds.

God will bring a revival in which we will clearly experience victory over our enemy as it happened when He parted the Red Sea, and the enemies of His people were buried under the sea. God will bring a revival that will proceed from covenant and obedience to His Word. It will not be just an emotional revival. It will be a revival based on His Word and will lead us to an authentic renewal of our covenant with our God and a total commitment to Him and His kingdom. As in Sinai, God will reveal Himself and will make known His glory and His splendor.

As when His people crossed the Jordan, He will

bring a revival for the salvation of the world. We have already begun to see it, and it will grow. The prophecy—telling that the Spirit will be poured out on all flesh, and that every knee shall bow and every tongue confess that Jesus Christ is Lord—will be fulfilled.

As the sun and the moon stood still because of one godly man's prayers, so the Lord will bring a victorious revival with signs and wonders to remind us that God is fighting for us.

Based on the Book of Habakkuk we can be sure that God will fulfill His promises. His Word is sure: "According to the oaths of the tribes, even thy word" (Hab. 3:9, KJV). God is simply fulfilling His promises to His people. God doesn't lie. God is not man or son of man to lie. His word is *yes* and *amen*. His promises are *yes* and *amen*.

God is the same yesterday and today and forever (Heb. 13:8). This world's circumstances change all the time, but God is over and above every circumstance: "But the LORD is in his holy temple; let all the earth be silent before him" (Hab. 2:20).

When the prophet stopped complaining and looked at his God, he remembered what the Lord had done for His people before, and his heart was changed. From the bitterness of the powerless complaint, he moved into the joy of the one who can perceive his future in a totally different way, because his God doesn't change, and His desire to act on behalf of His people is the same.

The prophet left his anguish behind. Beholding the Almighty, the God of all miracles, he stood in awe and began to rejoice. An indescribable confidence filled his heart, and he understood that from that moment on he could face the most adverse circumstance with joy, knowing that the Lord would give Him victory.

God's glory is the one that is at stake (3:3). God cannot be fooled or defeated. The whole earth will be full of His praise. God will send revival over all flesh, because He has decided that the whole earth will be filled with the knowledge of His glory, as the waters cover the sea (2:14). He has determined before the creation of the world, when the times will have reached their fulfillment, to bring all things in heaven and on earth together under Christ, in order that we might be for the praise of His glory. (See Ephesians 1:3–14.) It is His glory that is at stake.

The prophet declares: "For the revelation awaits an appointed time; it speaks of the end and will not prove false. Though it linger, wait for it; it will certainly come and will not delay" (Hab. 2:3). A revival is coming to the earth. Not because we deserve it, but because of God's infinite grace. The people of Judah, immediate recipients of this promise, deserved to be punished and oppressed. But God promised them a revival out of His love for them. He will do great things for us out of His love for His church, and especially because of His love for the lost. He will make Jesus' work known to all the peoples to the ends of the earth.

The Potter wants to make us jars of glory, vessels that will make His glory known to the world. Christ, the precious treasure, is present in our lives. Our simple jars of clay contain an incredible treasure within. Will the splendor of His glory flow out from our hearts to everyone lost, to everyone in need? He is restoring our lives, not for us to be satisfied with a fresh new touch of His Spirit, but for us to be channels of His revival. And it all begins with prayer.

... being confident of this, that he who began a good work in you will carry it on to completion until the day of Christ Jesus.

—Philippians 1:6

20

Final Words

FOR MANY YEARS my ministry was a vast desert. There was no fruit. Our little church at Parque Chas was empty. My fellow ministers were moving forward, but I seemed to be stuck. They were times of brokenness, times to die to myself. I had to learn to depend entirely on the Lord and grow in faith. All I could do was seek His face. Many times I thought of quitting, not finding the strength to go on, but the Potter was dealing with me.

One day, I went to visit Rafael Hiatt, a missionary very dear to us who had always encouraged us through the desert. I thought that if he could help us financially, we would be able to purchase a new church and evangelize the neighborhood. "You have the answer we need," I said. "If you send a letter to some ministry that can support us with funds for our project, then we will buy the new building and have an evangelistic crusade."

Rafael looked at me with eyes full of love, as always, and suddenly started to cry.

O great! I thought, *I've convinced him.* So I took the opportunity to remind him that I was battling alone and that nobody would come and help me. My seminary colleagues had prosperous churches and many were receiving support from other ministries, but not me.

Finally, after my long speech, Rafael looked at me and said, "Claudio, I would love to do this..."

"So, well, what are you waiting for?" I replied.

He continued, "...but unfortunately I can't do it." I could feel a lump in my throat. "Claudio, I do not sense that this is God's will. Pray to the Lord, and He will provide for you. Seek Him, and you will reach new heights. God is testing your faith. Do not rely on men; there is Someone who is all-sufficient and powerful, and your difficult circumstances can be changed only by Him."

After talking with Rafael for an hour and receiving his loving and tender words, I honestly have to say that I left that place even more frustrated than when I came. He had told me, "God is your source, seek Him." But I was desperately looking for a shortcut. Today, after many years, I can appreciate the wisdom of his words to me. Those years of apparent failure taught me a lot. When my own resources were finally exhausted, I discovered Christ as the source of my life, as my only hope.

I can bear testimony of how the Potter has been shaping my life. What seemed like failures, delays, steps back, He took as opportunities to place His hands on me, a jar of clay, to mold me according to His will. I have been able to see how the Bible promise has gradually become a reality in me: "Being confident of this, that he who began a good work in you will carry it on to completion until the day of Christ Jesus" (Phil. 1:6).

Your life may be barren and in need of restoration. My prayer is that as you were reading these pages, you allowed the Holy Spirit to perfect His work in you, touching you anew. I want to encourage you to put these words into action. I lovingly challenge you to make the right decisions from now on and to grow in communion with the Lord, guarding the anointing that has been renewed in you.

Allow me to give you a word of encouragement. We frequently hear the requirements of the Word of God, and we don't take into account the wonderful grace that comes along with it, enabling us to accomplish them. Don't try to do it on your own strength, but let the Holy Spirit fill you every day. Don't lose your thirst for Him. Don't try to seek God only when you find yourself in the midst of a crisis, but seek Him more and more each day.

Remember that even though you are clay, the

Potter took you, made you into a vessel and filled you so that you could become a jar of glory. Don't be satisfied with anything less than this!

We have an incredible treasure in jars of clay!

About the Author

Reverend Claudio Freidzon is the founder and current pastor of King of Kings Church (Iglesia Rey de Reyes), a part of the Assemblies of God in Buenos Aires, Argentina. His booming congregation of several thousand people is located in Belgrano, a neighborhood in the center of Buenos Aires.

Today God has called him and anointed him to minister, not only to his congregation, but also to churches, pastors and leaders from all over the world through several annual crusades and conferences.

He studied theology in the Instituto Biblico Río de la Plata (Río de la Plata Bible Institute), a school under the Assemblies of God. He graduated in 1977. He was a Bible teacher in several of the major seminaries. He went to graduate school at the Instituto de Superación Ministerial (ISUM), where he received a degree in theology. For several years in the city of Buenos Aires, he held the position of presbyter over all the congregations that are associated with the Assemblies of God.

In 1986 he founded King of Kings Church in Belgrano, where he developed a multiplying vision through training and evangelization cells, working toward the formation of leaders through an effective program of personal ministry and training. His goal is to reach the city and the whole nation with the gospel of Jesus Christ. In 1992, his personal search led him to a deep encounter with the Holy Spirit that revolutionized his life and ministry. A fresh anointing overflowed the meetings at King of Kings Church in an amazing and glorious way. Thousands of people from all over the world went there to be spiritually renewed.

He is the author of the book *Holy Spirit, I Hunger for You.* It has been translated into nine different languages. He also conducts several evangelistic programs on radio and television.

His ministry is characterized by a powerful manifestation of the Holy Spirit through signs and wonders and Christ-centered preaching in the light of the Scriptures. He has reached more than two million people all over the world through conferences and crusades.

Wherever he preaches, the end results are conversions, testimonies of miracles and deep spiritual renewal in pastors and lay people alike.

TO CONTACT HIM:

Rev. Claudio Freidzon

Iglesia Rey de Reyes-Ministerio a las Naciones-
Olaz·bal 2547 – (1428) Buenos Aires
República Argentina
Fax: 05411-47890047
E-mail: reydere@ibm.net

You can experience more of *God's grace* & *love!*